ALASKA HUNTING

Earthworms to Elephants

JAKE JACOBSON

Since 1978

PO Box 221974 Anchorage, Alaska 99522-1974
books@publicationconsultants.com—www.publicationconsultants.com

ISBN 978-1-59433-404-7

eBook ISBN Number: 978-1-59433-408-4

Library of Congress Catalog Card Number: 2013912497

J.P."Jake" Jacobson
Alaska Master Guide #54
PO Box 1313
Kodiak, Alaska 99615
website: www.huntfish.us/
email: huntfish@ak.net

Cover Photo by Bess Jacobson

Manufactured in the United States of America.

Contents

Foreword

Jake Jacobson is a true Alaskan legend…so it's a little strange that I first met him on a mountain above the Arizona desert. But maybe not so strange, because winter in Arizona is a lot more pleasant than winter in Alaska! But, strange or not, I first met James P.—just call me "Jake"—Jacobson while hunting Coues deer north of Tucson with our mutual friend Duwane Adams (himself a legend among Arizona hunters).

It's amazing how time flies. That was more than thirty years ago. We're all a bit older. Jake and I are both redheads, but his signature beard is showing a bit more silver than red these days. Maybe mine would, too, if I had the capability to grow one…but, as a favorite actor and director said, "A man's got to know his limitations." Even thirty years ago I didn't have enough time left to match Jake's whiskers!

For me it's been a busy life in a busy world and I have few regrets, but one of them is not having—or taking—more time to spend with people whose company I've enjoyed, and who I admire. Jake Jacobson is one of those people and, oddly, Duwane Adams who introduced us is another. But life is funny that way. Through various circumstances you can be with a person almost constantly, but never consider him or her a friend—and you can have genuine friends that you see only rarely. I feel privileged to have long considered Jake Jacobson such a friend.

I do have sort of an unspoken pact with the many guides and outfitters I've known over the years: They do what they do, and I do what I do. Meaning: They do the guiding and outfitting; I write the stories. Jake is not the first to have broken that pact (and probably not the last)…but I'm glad that he did. He is, in fact, and not just because I call him such, an Alaskan legend. Unlike me, a simple scribe, Jake has a story to tell…and it turns out that he tells it very well. As he should.

I've been a writer for a very long time now (I never said a good writer, but I've made my living at it since before I met Jake). Although I do indeed have an English degree, one of the things I think I have learned is that good writing doesn't come from fancy schools; it's more a knack than a skill, and I'm not sure it's a skill that can be learned. On the other hand, despite "spell check" and "grammar check," in this day and age a prospective writer is better off knowing how to write a straight sentence. Jake Jacobson, Alaskan Master Guide Number 54 (a low number) is actually an educated man. More to the point, he is far more educated than I!

He is, in fact, a doctor of dentistry, one of three legends in Alaskan guiding who, essentially, came north to fix teeth and go hunting...and stayed for the hunting. The other two, both friends of Jake's, are Tony Oney and Jim "Hoppy" Harrower. Like Tony and Hoppy a few years earlier, Jake learned Alaska by traveling throughout the new state, giving dental care to villages that rarely see a real dentist. But even then, in 1967, he was already an Assistant Guide, the first step in Alaska's hierarchy. In 1972 his status improved to Registered Guide, and in 1984 he made the lofty step to Master Guide (Number 54). As we said in the military, that's a "terminal rank" with no further promotion possible. In time Jake forsook dentistry for outfitting but, as you'll see in this collection of stories, he retained the innate knack for telling a story...and the learned skill to write a straight sentence.

Aside from technical skills, however, there is one more ingredient required for a writer: He must have a story to tell. Novelists make them up, and I admire (and envy) their imagination. The rest of us can only tell true stories, our own or someone else's. In this book Jake tells his own story. He tells it well, with both knack and skill...and his is an enviable story to tell. He hit Alaska at a good time, shortly after statehood, and he matured with modern Alaska—which remains radically different from the Lower 48.

He is not the first longtime Alaskan guide to write his memoirs, and I'm quite sure he will not be the last. But as I think you will see, very few have retold the journey with as much fun as Jake Jacobson. Elsewhere in this volume he will tell about my short journey on the doomed ship Leprechaun...Oh, Lord, I don't think I take myself too seriously, but I don't expect practical jokes before the hunt even starts.

And then there was the day when we were working our way along a steep hillside. We took a break beside a bubbling brook—I was more than ready for a breather, but there was no way I could ask for one, so I was relieved when Jake shrugged off his pack and bent down to take a drink. Then he got excited, digging furiously in the sand and triumphantly showing me the small gold nugget he had captured.

It's Alaska, there's gold in every stream (and mastodon tusks at every bend). Greed is an amazing force, and I bought into it for several seconds too long. Then I got it. He's a dentist; he works with gold. He has fillings-in-training to salt (from a vial in his shirt pocket) for gullible pilgrims. We had a good laugh and we moved on. And that's the beauty of this collection of stories of the Alaskan wilderness. Some are funny, some are serious, and some are scary…so you'll laugh, cry, and shiver…and then you'll move on. And long before you're done you will understand why James P. "Jake" Jacobson, Alaskan Master Guide Number 54, truly deserves the oft-bestowed, but rarely earned, title of legend.

Craig Boddington
Elk City, Kansas
June 2013

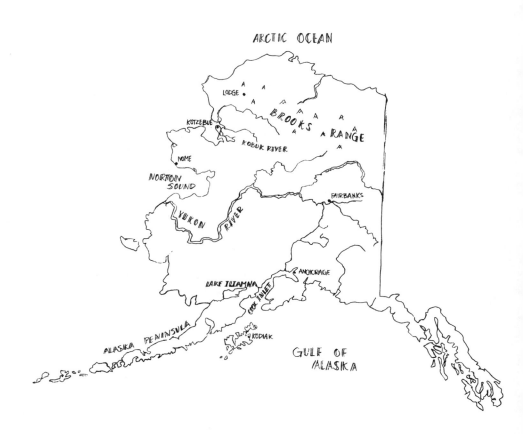

Map credit: Jenelle Bess Jacobson

Writing this collection
of short stories

So many times I have been told by others that they planned to write a book. In most cases, I was anxious to see what they had to say. In very few cases did they actually ever write anything at all. I, too, considered writing a book, but avoided mentioning it, as I didn't want to join the ranks of those whose deeds did not match their words. Besides, everyone has their own life stories. Why would mine be of interest to anyone but myself?

I had the pleasure of taking Patrick McManus, the great American outdoor humor writer, fishing in my boat *F/V LADY SASQUATCH*, a few years back. The time we spent together was totally delightful. In person, he was just as the character described in his stories.

I asked him about writing, which he was teaching at Eastern Washington State University in Spokane. He said, in his case, writing did not come easily. He sequestered himself in his room, forbidding any interruptions and hammered his stuff out, word by word. He was personally very disciplined, unlike most of his characters.

A story of his fishing trip with my sister and me appeared in Outdoor Life and I emailed him a spoofy attempt at communicating in his type of humor. He was most generous in his comments to me.

In the dozen or so years that have passed since that day with Patrick, I have tortured myself with the idea of writing a book. Where would I begin? How could I string a collection of some of the significant parts of my life together, making it worthwhile for others to spend time reading? Like most of life, the answer to that question was fairly simple. Just as we gut and clean fish and rabbits one at a time, I would write my stories, one at a time. I would focus on short stories, rather than any sort of novel or autobiography. A bite at a time - hopefully properly chewed before swallowing.

Some of my friends, amateur would-be writers, too, told me how rigorous the process of using an editor and actually getting the book into print had proved to be. Months or years might be required. Costs escalated as the time spent on their project dragged on.

I resolved to not have anything printed just to satisfy my ego If I could invest a reasonable amount of time and money and have a chance at breaking even, well, I just might do that.

I've always been aware of how lucky and blessed I am. I owed a lot for my good fortune and thought a recounting of tales might be a means of partial pay back for the wonderful life I have been granted.

Okay, so I began writing things down.

I began to purchase books on writing. I found such books on the internet, in used book stores, at yard sales and at the Salvation Army. My writers' library expanded faster than I could properly study it. Punctuation, format, conjugation (is that legal in your state...between relatives?)...etc. It sounded like a series of unfamiliar, terrible nightmares. I was enjoying recounting my experiences primarily from memory, augmented by my collection of photographs, home movies, videos and, most of all, my personal logs (they are **not** diaries, by golly!) which I had kept faithfully for more than fifty years. Writing was fun. However it looked like preparations for publishing would be less than entertaining.

The situation reminded me of when, in a weak moment, I let a physician spook me into going to the Emergency Room. After telling me of the worst case scenario...yeah, I might die...the Doctor told me I was going to have to take Medivac flight to Anchorage. That's reportedly an $80,000 dollar plane trip from Kodiak! He said they needed a biopsy from my lung. I asked if it would be a needle biopsy. He said they would have to open it. I asked "Open what?" He said, "Your chest!" Hearing that, I stood up an said "No way, I'm going home...now!" The nurse told me that I couldn't leave without release orders from the Doctor. I told the nurse that I was never their prisoner and in one hour I would no longer be their patient. I went home, and so far, am still alive...last time I checked.

So, one day I reasoned that as people seemed to be able to understand most of what I express in word or script, well then, I would plan to write my stuff as I speak, then see what it would cost to get it into soft cover book form. I would do it by the seat of my pants, as I have done so many things in my life. It seemed that I could perhaps escape jumping through the hoops and protocols of others, as I have always tried to do. Why not set my own protocols? I planned to wing it.

Mea culpa if my punctuation, syntax, constuction, grammar, photo quality and other aspects of my amateurish attempt to entertain readers do not meet their standards. But I can grasp the meaning of most of my own words and I hope other readers can, too. Anyway, that may just have to be good enough.

In my attempt to entertain, some of my stuff is off the cuff corny, as intended by me, but some comes across dull and flat due to my ineptitude and sometimes dull nature. One can't fix stupid, but it can be admitted and apologies made. Please forgive me.

Reader beware, this collection of stories may offend, disgust or bore you. Be prepared to cast it aside, maybe use it for fire starter or to line the bottom of a canary cage. But I hope that for at least a few, it may prove to be of some quantifiable value. Titillating, even…maybe.

Jake Jacobson - 2013
Kodiak and Kotzebue
website: www. huntfish.us/
email: huntfish@ak.net

Earthworms in Alaska

Often - whenever I got the chance, actually - as a kid and young man, I hunted up anything that might be used as fish or trap bait. If I was not planning to go fishing or had a surplus, older people or other kids were happy to buy my catch. Earth worms were much easier to keep alive than the other bugs…and they didn't sting or spit tobacco juice on me.

In the desert areas grasshoppers or crickets were the main fish bait. In desperate times we occasionally used scorpions from which we had pinched off the stinger. On one occasion I wrestled a tarantula onto my hook which was immediately swallowed by a five pound large mouth bass.

A large desert centipede tempted me. I figured that writhing, wiggling, hyper active bug would be a sure draw for big fish, but after a few minutes of trying to find a way to hook it without being impaled by either end of the insect or by my own fishing hook, I cut off both ends, divided the long body into six pieces and found those still writhing sections worked very well on crappie. But I preferred the docile earthworms, as did my fishing companions.

Digging worms was a welcome diversion from my heavy work and study schedule while attending dental school in Portland. A fellow student introduced me to the technique of placing a copper pipe in the ground, then hooking it up to a twelve volt battery, which brought the big night crawlers oozing up out of the grass. Such easy catching it was—a technological triumph!

So when I got to Alaska, I missed some things, like ring necked pheasant hunting, my previous easy access to horses and burros, and worming.

On my first trip to Kodiak in October, 1967, while looking over a small midtown lake I noticed fish activity. In a moment of reminiscence I turned over a half rotten log and discovered earthworms.

Immediately I knew I was home!

Wife, Teresa and daughters ate what they harvested.

Kate, me and Bess with an early harvest.

Kids' Hunting and Fishing

Kids should be started out early on things that are most important in life, and I believe being provident and self sufficient are at the top of the list. Making use of locally available fish and game resources requires hunting and fishing. Both activities are also great fun, so I began to involve our kids in such pursuits before they could walk. By the time they had their own single shot rifles, they were well on the way to a hunting life.

Living in Kodiak since birth, with trips to the lodge in the arctic before school started in the fall, hunting and fishing has been easily accessible to our daughters and they accepted those activities as a normal part of their everyday lives. Proper preparation of the animals taken was required, with the whole family lending a hand. Family involvement was always our first priority.

Nature's bounty was always at hand, sometimes more abundantly than other periods, but always available in usable forms. The seasonal and annual vagaries of nature and animal availability are realities that all people should come to expect and accommodate.

Constant availability of store bought food is an artificial aspect of modern urbanized life and one should not be overly dependent upon having access to such extraneous resources. My family eats mainly wild meat.

My wife and I have always emphasized these truths when raising our children.

My Grandparents, Then Being Grampa

My paternal grandparents, Grant Victor and Minnie Jacobson, fit the bill and filled the shoes of their honorific titles as well as could be done. I simply could not have had better paternal grandparents.

My Mom's mother was a sterling example of how a Grandma should be, also.

Grandpa Jacobson spent a lot of time showing me how to tie lines, fish, hunt small game and just about everything a young boy should know. He made sure that I carried a decent pocket knife and kept it sharp, which I still do. I still retain a clear mental picture of his hands. He had great looking hands. I watched him use them on so many things that turned out so well.

Grandma made sure I knew how to kill and pluck chickens, clean fish and weed the garden, among other less interesting chores. I realized how lucky I was and resolved to try my best to come as close to providing that quality of love and attention to my kids and grand kids, as I could, when and if, God willing, my turn came around. And, eventually, my turn did come.

Our family tends to "daughter out" with fewer male progeny than those of the female gender, so initially I had granddaughters to take fishing and we focused on that, with both winter and summer trips.

It was always a special pleasure to hear the squeals of excitement and watch the struggles of the grand kids as they brought their fish to the beach. Cooking the fresh catch, wrapped in aluminum foil with lemon pepper, on a bed of willow coals always drew their attention and anticipation of a tasty outdoor meal. It was living off the land, and it left us all with indelible memories.

When all is said and done, life is primarily a collection of memories and we ought to all work to make ours primarily good ones.

Family fishin' on a beautiful July day in the Arctic.

Spencer with a beautiful winter killed Moose rack.

Then, some grandsons showed up. Spencer, the oldest, immediately showed a keen interest in hunting. When he was five years old, we made our first overnight trip, hunting for moose and ducks. A few small ducks were all we put in the bag, but the trip was wonderful. After setting up the tent and making a suitable fireplace, we crept along the lake shore and Spencer was able to pot shoot a couple of quackers with his single shot .410. Before dark, we had two ducks plucked, singed, seasoned and laid out on the grill. The fat sizzled and popped as it dripped onto the coals. A very attractive set of Moose horns from a winter killed bull were nearby, adding to the marvels of the day.

A large Black Spruce tree rose from a small knoll a bit further down the lake shore from our camping spot. As we returned to the camp site, Spencer walked over to the landmark tree and noticed some long scars running from about eight feet up the trunk to three feet from the bottom. All were weeping fresh pitch. He asked me what had made them and I told him that a very large grizzly had stretched up to scratch the tree and, from the appearance, it had happened several times. Some of the scratches were recently done. This was a marking tree, delineating the bear's territory. My grandson was silently contemplative.

At last light, we hear the distant howling of wolves. Their voices sounded mournful and eerie, followed by the insane call of an Arctic Loon. Spencer's eyes were wide open and I thought I noticed his ears perk up, too, - but maybe I just imagined that.

I told Spencer that most boys his age had never had and never would have such an experience, such as the wilderness sounds in a truly pristine, remote place. City kids just don't know what they are missing. He said "Uh huh."

After sundown, as we ate the ducks, especially savoring the crispy skin, along with stick bread and fresh berries, I mentioned that I had never tasted better and could think of no place that I would rather be, than where we were, just then. Spencer nodded in agreement.

We crawled into our down sleeping bags and tucked in for the night about 10:00 pm. As usual for me, soon after my head hit my wadded up jacket which I used for a pillow, I was asleep. At 2:30am I was awakened by Spencer gently nudging me and whispering "Grampa, Grampa!"

Our tent camps were simple, cooking on an open fire.

I rolled over and asked "What is it Spence?"

He questioned, "What kind of sound does a Grizzly Bear make?"

I replied that they normally don't make any sound at all.

He said, "I think I just heard one! Where's your pistol?"

I realized that he had been awake ever since we hit the sacks, likely thinking of the deep scratches on the spruce tree and the monster that had made them.

I assured Spencer that my .44 Magnum was right between us and that we would both keep a close listen, just in case, but that we also needed to get some sleep, so we'd be ready to look for moose at sunup.

Soon, I dozed off back to sleep, but from the look of Spencer in the morning, he did not sleep at all that night.

Ancient Artifacts
Wooly Mammoth Tusks

Wooly mammoth tusks and teeth are found throughout northern and interior Alaska near thawing permafrost areas and eroding stream banks. Hydraulic gold mining released many from the permafrost in the Fairbanks and Nome areas. Often they were cast aside at the diggings, to later be sold to dealers or others.

In my travels about the state I had seen many very impressive examples of the extinct elephants dentition. I dreamed that someday I might find one myself. I'd heard lots of stories of tusks being seen on lake bottoms or just lying about on the tundra. Most stories ended with the lucky finder being unable to retrieve the prize for various reasons. Most commonly they could not relocate the site. I found it incredible that such an astounding attraction could be left unrecovered, whatever the circumstances. I knew that I would move mountains, if necessary, to secure any such find that ever came my way.

In June of 1971 my wife, Mae, and I were flying from Kotzebue to Buckland to provide field dental services and to purchase some dried smelt. Kotzebue Sound was still full of large pans of winter ice and we observed many seals enjoying the sun atop the ice, when I realized that we really should be checking out the permafrost cut banks along the coast in case the thawing conditions might have given up something interesting.

The area we were flying through had been an ancient river delta and this is the type of place that commonly surrenders parts of ancient animals. It is assumed that carcasses were washed down current until they grounded, then were covered in silt and muck, and eventually frozen in place. On rare occasions some hide and hair is found along with the bones or teeth.

The tusk was about 120 feet above the beach.

The tusk as we saw it from the air.

Wooly mammoths became extinct about 10,000 years ago on mainland Alaska, but recent discoveries indicate that a few probably survived on Wrangel Island until about the time of Christ.

I banked the Cessna to the left and immediately upon intersecting the coast I saw what appeared to be a log protruding from a melted area of permafrost. However I had never before seen a log in these cliffs. Closer inspection revealed it to be a Wooly Mammoth tusk! We couldn't believe our eyes, or our luck!

I dropped full flaps and soared by it several times. YES, it was a tusk. I memorized some terrane features to enable me to come back to the same spot and began to plan how to retrieve that dandy, intact chunk of ivory. We completed the trip to Buckland, but the tusk was foremost on my mind. I had to get it before anyone else stumbled onto it!

On the way home I looked the area over carefully, found a spot suitable for landing the Cessna 180 and since we had a light load, I landed to check it out more closely. With a little clean up, I felt I could safely land and take off from there with a heavier load in the plane. As soon as I got in the house I called a couple of friends, asking if they would like to take part in the recovery. They both jumped at the opportunity.

Mae, my "anchor man" and me.

A few days later, in perfect weather, I landed the plane with Mae and my two buddies. I brought along some ropes and a pickax with which I intended to chop loose the frozen muck on the lower end of the tusk, allowing it to break free. Two ropes were to hold the exposed ends of the tusk, to keep it, hopefully, from breaking as it fell. The other rope was secured to a stake and watched by my "anchor man" was to hold me next to the face of the bank allowing me to chop the frozen Pleistocene muck to free the prize.

However, due to the position of the tusk, I had to hang below it to chop. I hung onto the rope with my left hand, sitting on a piece of wood, rigged like a swing seat, and swung the ax with my right. Each blow would project me away from the bank and most of the force of the chopping resulted in me swinging, rather than removing the frozen muck. That permafrost was tough and unyielding. After two hours of tiring, frustrating effort, I needed to rest and think. I wasn't going to leave without the tusk.

As always I had a rifle in the plane for protection from Grizzlies which are found everywhere throughout the region. This time I had a 30:06 with 220 grain bullets. I began shooting the permafrost holding the tusk in place. It was very effective. After eight shots, the last clump of frozen muck blew off and the tusk came loose. The ropes cushioned it's fall and we had it!

It measured exactly seven feet in length and weighed 70 pounds. A female wooly mammoth had carried this enlarged canine on her left side.

We scoured the area for the other tusk and any other bones. I was half way expecting to find the other side, as well as the skull, but the one tusk was all we could locate.

This thawing site smelled like a horse barn. We had a big enough load for the plane given the length and condition of the strip, so we did not take any of the thawed muck for the garden, but I gave it some thought. Prehistoric fertilizer might add something special to our turnips!

It had been a 14 hour day by the time we got home. But what a day!

Over the years, I located 12 wooly mammoth tusks and recovered them all, but the first one was the best, - and required the greatest planning and effort to retrieve. It was in great condition and intact. About 20 years later I saw what I am sure was the right tusk to match the one we recovered. It was for sale in Kotzebue for $10,000. I did not attempt to purchase it.

The Raven's Perch

In September,1976 as I was flying a German guest hunter to the lodge, which at that time was still just a small cabin, but we encountered severe weather and turned back. This fellow had already completed a guided hunt in Alaska, but had not been successful and contacted me. He wanted to take some trophies before he returned to the Fatherland. His time was short, so rather than fly all the way back to Kotzebue, only to retrace our journey the next morning ,I decided to land on a river bar and spend the night in the tent. It was late in the evening and with the heavy overcast, light was poor. I swung wide on my approach to the intended landing area and saw a raven perched on what appeared to be a stump sticking up from the tundra.

As that area was bare tundra, with no trees, something seemed wrong with what I'd seen. I banked and turned toward the raven, which was still sitting. Sure enough…it was the butt end of a wooly mammoth tusk! I made some mental landmarks and told the German what we had seen. He wanted to forget about his hunt and go get that tusk, but I told him that it was stuck deep into permafrost and with the current freezing weather, we would only destroy it if we tried to get it out. Besides, he had not booked for elephant!

The ravens perch, thrust up by a frost heave.

The following summer I easily relocated the tusk. It was still there, but more difficult to see without the raven to mark it. It's a wonder that I ever noticed it initially, especially in the dim light of that stormy evening. This time I took the super cub on floats and an ax. First I chopped away the tundra, exposing the underlying permafrost and left it to thaw.

About a week later I had a charter to a nearby spot and landed to check the tusk. It was still firmly locked in the ice. I decided to expedite this tooth extraction with a propane heater. In a few days I was back with a heater, ax and hand tools. I removed that tusk after a few hours of cooking and shoveling out the smelly muck - hard work. This tusk was broken and about a foot and a half of the end was missing. If I had been more patient, I believe the summer heat would have done all that work for me.

An Easy Pick Up on a Beach

We always kept our eyes peeled when flying, looking for shed antlers, washed up walrus carcasses, tusks, or whatever else might show up. Once, coming home from an ivory buying trip for Mae's store, Arctic Rivers Trading Company, she spotted a large tusk sticking out of the sand on a

Mae with Wooly Mammoth bull tusk on a beach.

Some of the tusks we found.

beach beneath a thawing cut bank. It was simply a case of finding a suitable landing spot in the soft sand of the beach and walking a few hundred yards to the tusk to dig it out and carry it back to the cub. This tusk, like most we found, was not intact, but it's ivory would provide wonderful material for local artisans to use for making jewelry. Wooly mammoth ivory varies from the original white to various shades of blue or brown, depending on the color and minerals in the muck it has been buried in for centuries. Polished and/or etched, it is beautiful and unique to Alaska.

An Immature Mammoth Tusk, Chopped By Man

It is generally accepted that Wooly Mammoths became extinct in North America about ten thousand years ago.

Several years ago I saw an immature mammoth tusk mounted on a slab of a mature tusk that seems to show chop marks on both sides of the "root" end. It appears that the small tusk was removed from the surrounding bone by using a stone age adz or other primitive cutting tool. I've never seen another like it, but it clearly poses the question of how recently mankind in Alaska interacted with and probably dined on Wooly Mammoths. I may have an opportunity to get this small tusk aged using the radiocarbon technique.

A Steppe Bison

Enroute back to Kotzebue from points south one beautiful spring morning I was flying low, varying my altitude between 50 and 100 feet to "grow and shrink" a mirage on the horizon. It is an unusual phenomenon, occasionally demonstrable in clear, cold conditions. I was entertained by it. As I passed

"Chop marks" on an immature Wooly Mammoth tusk.

Steppe Bison became extinct about 10,000 years ago.

a large bluff, hollowed out by the melting of permafrost, I saw a large skull and one horn lying midway up a recently fallen pile of muck.

Wow, that was the first one of those that I had stumbled upon! I had a large load of dental gear, but was light on fuel. Just offshore I saw a flat spot of ice to land the cub and looked it over at low speed. It was not the smoothest spot I had seen, but it looked like it should be okay. When my skis touched the ice, it was plenty noisy as the machine glided over some broken ice, but my beefed up axles did their job and I hopped out, then put my engine cover on.

A pair of Arctic Foxes had left their prints around the skull. I wondered if they had some sort of ancient, intergenerational memory of feeding on kin of this bull.

I carefully searched for the right horn, but after half an hour, found no sign of it. I returned several times over the next few months, in hopes of finding the missing horn, but I was not successful.

The cub, that day, was stuffed with four apple boxes of dental gear, my folding field chair and foam pad, compressor, emergency gear and food. I dug out a small rope and tied the head to the wing struts for the trip home. Picking up prizes doesn't get much easier than that. Talk about charismatic megafauna!

2012, The Fall Season

The fall season did not begin well, but it sure could have been a lot worse. After getting the super cub annual done without any complications - other than a twenty foot strip of leading edge fabric delaminating from the left wing during my biannual flight check. Lucky for me, the check pilot was the mechanic who just signed off on the annual. I replaced it with about three hours of cutting and gluing in the hanger.

Then, as so often happens, a huge storm moved in, obscuring visibility from Fairbanks to Kotzebue. Oh well, I spent three days shopping for hard to find items, visiting with friends and doing some reading.

It was an enjoyable time delay - nothing unusual.

Having checked the forecast at the Flight Service Station the evening before, I did not expect to fly at all that Saturday, but I rolled up my sleeping bag and got ready, just in case. Upon calling up the new charts, I was surprised to see what looked like a narrow window between two large low pressure systems that, if the storms moved as predicted, would allow me to slip across the 440 miles separating where I was from where I wanted to be. If I didn't make it through that narrow window, I would probably be delayed for several more days.

I decided it was good enough for a go.

I stopped at a convenience store to fill my coffee thermos and grab a mini pecan pie. That with my bread, ham and cheese would do fine until I get to Kotzebue. I always carry emergency rations for a trip like that as well.

At Chena Marina airstrip I loaded the cub, topped of the main tanks and filled the belly tank, giving me fuel enough for eight and a half hours of flight time. I also had my "range extender" a plastic bottle that supplements my internal bladder - necessary for long cross country flights without any stops. Once, when able to make the flight directly, it took only four and a quarter hours, but I have spent over eight and a half hours on that same trip. The average direct flight takes about six to six and a half hours. The cramped misery would be multiplied, and my bladder unduly stressed, without a range extender.

The first fifty miles went very well. I trimmed the plane for best rate of climb - 72 mph airspeed - and as I ascended past 3,000 feet, my instruments indicated that the quartering left cross wind translated into about a five to eight mile per hour tail wind. That's like money in the bank and reduces the need for frequent use of the range extender, which is a somewhat uncomfortable maneuver from the front seat of a super cub. Performing what for men is normally a stand-up job from a cramped, seated position requires some well practiced contortions, but it beats the alternative. I imagine a monkey attempting to mount a stiff hair brush while in a washing machine, might be a more graceful sight.

I tuned in my thirty -five year old Automatic Direction Finder (ADF), picked up a Fairbanks radio station and listened to country western music.

Everything going well, I poured myself a cup of coffee and munched down a ham and cheese sandwich, then the pecan pie.

Before I reached the Yukon River I began to encounter light turbulence accompanied by heavy rain. Visibility was good, so I locked onto a GPS heading of 268 degrees, and kept grinding directly westward.

It was warm when I departed Fairbanks - about plus sixty-eight degrees, but as I gained altitude the outside air temperature dropped to plus thirty-four. Wearing only a cotton shirt and having nothing handy to put over that, I pulled the heat lever and the cabin soon was comfortable from steady airflow pouring from the flexible heater hose. Once I was warmed up I stuck the heater hose under my seat. The warm air blowing up my butt felt good and reminded me of previous attendances at political meetings. Citizen voters are expected to feel good with hot air blowing up their butt...right? It happens in a small aircraft, too.

After about two hours my direct course took me to the Koyukuk river just downstream from the village of Hughs, but the wind blowing from 140 degrees had become stronger and was now steady at an estimated 35-40 mph with higher gusts as visibility dropped to about five miles.

Moderate turbulence was steadily thumping me. If I had brought along some dirty laundry in a sealable container with soap it would have received a thorough cycling, - even without an internal agitator.

Realizing that the wind boiling over the mountains west of the Hog River gold mine would make for a really bumpy ride and noticing that the upper half of the mountains was obscured, I flew through the Babantaltlin Hills, then diverted my route to south of the Hogatza range.

It was time to again relieve the bladder before conditions became too demanding for such a distraction, so I did so. It's best to have a bit of altitude and manageable flight command circumstances for such a pretzeling endeavor.

That wind out of the Southeast produced an updraft as it smacked into the terrane, causing me to trim the cub a bit nose down to keep from being pushed up into the overcast and now I was clocking along with my ground speed indicated at 125 mph, a full twenty to thirty-one miles faster than my airspeed. All was good.

Wheeler Creek leads one northwest up a broad, treeless valley to the head of the Selawik River. That route is a "no-no" in overcast conditions during winter time due to the potential for white-outs. With no trees, the snowy surface can be extremely difficult to see. Today there was no snow, but the rain squalls were so large and dense that I elected to continue on my tack south of the Purcell Mountains. The ceiling and visibility kept dropping, but I needed only about fifteen hundred feet to clear the southern edge of the hills and reach the Selawik flats, so I stayed the course.

Clearing the ridge with a couple hundred feet to spare, I dropped into the flats. Visibility continued to deteriorate and I was getting head winds which reduced my ground speed to 78 mph. The extra thirty-two gallons in the belly tank provide a great comfort on any long flight.

Fog went all the way to the ground in places, so I steered north to the winding Selawik River and followed it downstream.

I was able to pick up the Kotzebue Non-Directional Beacon (NDB) about 150 miles out on my ADF and the broadcast indicated conditions were below VFR minimums at that station. I tuned my VHF radio to the Ambler frequency and called to check the weather, but got no response. I switched to the Selawik frequency and again did not make contact. The ceiling remained steady at about 800 feet and visibility varied from less than a mile to about two miles, so I continued on, figuring that if the Kotzebue airport was below minimums when I arrived I could hold outside the control zone for a good while until things got better or I might even land on the beach at Riley Wreck or Seshaulik, each of which is less than ten miles from Kotzebue. The belly tank full of extra fuel is such a wonderful thing.

My ADF audio was functioning and I noted that conditions were close to those allowing for a "special VFR clearance" to enter the zone and land, so as I crossed Hotham Inlet I called in my position again on the VHF radio and asked for a clearance, hoping to be heard.

"Kotzebue radio, Piper 3421 Papa - west shore inbound, request Special VFR clearance', I said.

That transmission was heard by the Kotzebue Flight Service Station (FSS) and I was given clearance.

"Jake, Kotzebue radio, good to hear you, cleared to enter the zone", or some such thing. I noted that my name was used, rather than my "N" number. Familiarity has its advantages.

When I was able to see Kotzebue the wind was blowing Southeast - still 140 degrees at 25 gusting to 38 knots. My rotating beacon, navigation, landing and taxi lights were all on. No other aircraft occupied the zone.

I advised Kotzebue radio that I was on short base leg for runway 180 and intended to land long. My transmission was not answered. My radio was non functional, again.

As I crabbed toward the threshold of the south runway with the wind blowing from the left, I allowed the plane to drift a bit to the right of the dirt landing strip. This would allow me to correct a wee bit to the left to slightly reduce the angle of cross wind. Cross winds tend to make aircraft weathercock or turn into the wind, which is counter acted by dropping the upwind aileron fully, lowering the wing on that side and using the opposite brake as required to hold the roll out straight. Normally one lands on the main wheels, keeping the tail wheel off the ground for better control.

An especially heavy rain squall had reduced visibility and I could not see half way down the runway when my wheels touched. As I let the tail wheel come into contact with the gravel, the cub veered hard to the right which is the opposite of what I expected. I was heading rapidly for the sewer pond just off the right side of the strip. I jammed my heel down hard on the left brake which brought the plane sharply to the left - but with too much speed. I nearly ground looped the aircraft, but luckily did not scrape the right wing tip or otherwise damage the plane. Then I was headed for the ditch on the upwind side of the strip, however the plane was slowing down. I rode both brakes hard with the control stick full back in my lap and came to a stop just short of the drop off. All this action took place in mere seconds, but my mind had traveled through the entire flight training book.

Had I forgotten how to land the durned thing?

I popped open the clam shell door, leaving the engine running on idle, and got out. In the heavy rain I grabbed the handle near the tail and pushed the plane back onto the runway. As I got back in I noticed steam coming from beneath my seat. The driving rain had hit my two brake master cylinders which were so hot they were producing the steam. I'd left the heater hose nozzle right next to the brake cylinders and the fluid had expanded, causing my brakes to be firmly locked. This explained my wild landing. I had never heard of such a thing, but everyone I encountered heard the story from me. I hoped that no one else would make such an error. Whew! I nearly wrecked the cub three times on that one landing. I felt like I was riding in the palm of God's hand.

With the plane secured in its tie downs, my new priorities were bladder relief and emptying the range extender before anyone arrived to bear witness to either act.

My daughter, Sandy, came out to the field to help me unload and drive me to town. As we passed the FSS I stopped in to thank them for the clearance and make sure my flight plan was closed. I asked what they thought of my landing, but they said the visibility clamped down just before I landed and they had not been able to see my yellow and black cub much beyond the threshold. I was glad I had intentionally landed long. I did not elaborate on my touch down with the FSS attendants at the time.

Having arrived in Kotzebue on Saturday afternoon, it was sunup Thursday morning before I had conditions suitable enough for a trip to the lodge on Trail Creek. I made three trips with one passenger each time that day.

We found scant sign of snowshoe hares around the buildings, but that was likely explained by the presence of Lynx. Scat and scratch marks were evident in the yard and a large male cat was standing by the door as the first night fell. This was somewhat of a relief to me, as the hares can rebound from heavy predation, but disease can keep their numbers down for many years.

In the spring of 1980 we had more snowshoe hares than I have ever seen before or since, but in April they began to show a bloody diarrhea. I did not see another snowshoe until August, 2005.

The night we arrived rain showers began and continued for the next six days. We spent most of the time inside the buildings. It was not what we had come for, but much better than being stuck in Kotzebue.

The following Wednesday I transported one guest to Kotzebue and the following day met the two incoming guests. We sat until Saturday before weather conditions allowed me to get them to the lodge on September 1.

September second dawned with rain and fog. We enjoyed a hearty breakfast and as we lingered in the main room, someone spotted a herd of about one hundred and eighty Caribou coming down the east side of the valley. This band was comprised of mostly cows and calves with three young bulls and two large trophy bulls bringing up the rear. They had come out of Break Ankle Canyon and side-hilled just east of the lodge, almost within rifle range, but moving at a steady clip.

Ron and Brent took off across the swamp in hopes of getting a shot, but they returned after two hours. The animals were just moving too fast.

We were enjoying bowls of warm soup when I glassed a good bear feeding on berries on the north slope of Three Mile Ridge, down creek from the lodge. The rain had stopped and visibility was good. Our guest hunter, Brent, Ron and I set off immediately toward the bear.

We used walking sticks to assist in fording the rain swollen channels of Trail Creek, leaving them on the far bank. When we had walked to within a mile of the last known location of the bear, we could no longer see it. We sat near the bank of the stream, focused on the berry littered hillside until after about a half hour, Ron detected what he thought was the top of the bear's back. When I located his mark, I agreed that it was the bear, lying just across a small drainage. We struck off at a fast walk.

The wind was steady at ten to twelve miles per hour down the valley. We were upwind, but about two hundred feet lower elevation than the bear. I was confident that we could go straight for the bruin with little risk of it winding us.

Over the years I have come to realize that bears eyesight is much better than most people think. And all bears know their country well. To avoid exposing ourselves as we moved along the edge of an open alluvial fan, even though it was a half mile from the bear, we chose a route that forced us to claw our way across a steep, muddy cut bank of the river. A slip there would have landed us in the rushing water, but a glimpse of us skylined on the edge of the fan would surely have resulted in the bear disappearing into the heavily brush choked draw just beyond the meadow in which it was feeding.

The last thousand yards to the bear were mostly knee high brush with a few taller bushes and some shallow draws. We used the cover as best we could and finally were within 350 yards of the bear which was once again up and feeding.

We needed to close the range as much as possible, so I sent Ron in front with Brent close behind and me bringing up the rear, filming. We proceeded very slowly and stayed close behind each other in order to make only one silhouette, in case the bear looked our way and detected something amiss.

Daylight was threatening to close down our operation if the shot was not made soon. The dark Grizzly began to move more rapidly toward the brushy draw and was only one hundred yards from the cover when I told Brent he would have to make his shot. The range by then was around 225 yards. I recorded the event with my video camera. The sound of the first bullet impacting the bear was unmistakable. Immediately, the beast rolled and nipped at itself, not knowing what had bitten it. My impression was that the shot was a bit aft of ideal, a bit toward the stern side - euphemisms aside, it was a gut shot.

"Shoot him again, Brent," I hollered.

I sensed the second shot was a miss and told Ron to help. The wounded bear was running full stride for the heavy cover.

Once a bear has been hit, it is our practice to have the guest hunter keep shooting it until it lies motionless, or if it appears to be escaping, Ron or I may assist in putting it down.

The Grizzly disappeared into the tangled vegetation without another shot being fired.

Then I realized that both Ron and I had been filming. That was my mistake as I should have made sure that one of us was ready to shoot if necessary.

With the wind still steady from the north, I walked around the lower end of the brush and told Ron to take Brent to the upper end after giving me fifteen minutes to get set up on the downwind side. I was hoping that with rare good luck, the bear would smell the two men and come out downwind, allowing me to dispatch it. This bear, like most wounded bruins, remained holed up in the dense thicket.

After thirty minutes Ron left Brent in position with a good view, cautioning him to shoot only if the bear came out in the clear on his side, but under no circumstances was he to shoot toward the brushy draw.

When Ron and I met, I told him that there was time enough for me to make one criss crossing shashay down through the draw in hopes of locating the bear. If the bear was dead, we would have a difficult time finding it, but I was confident that it was gut shot and would be plenty lively...and angry. If I did not rouse the bear in one downhill transit we would have to come back in the morning.

"Boss, how 'bout I go through the brush with you?", asked Ron.

In my 45 years of guiding in Alaska I have dug numerous wounded bears out of dense thickets, but never allowed anyone to come along. I'd much rather risk a mauling than being shot by accident with a soft nosed hunting bullet. But this thicket was large and two people working it seemed a better idea, especially since Ron is cool natured and absolutely dependable.

"Ron, that is a capital idea! We should try to remain within twenty to thirty yards of each other and keep in frequent voice contact. The noise will no doubt hold the bear's attention and coming from two sources, I think it will confuse the beast and hopefully prevent it from making a well calculated rush on either of us. So, partner, let's do it!", I replied.

We each put a round in the chamber and checked that our magazines had three more.

I told Ron that in circumstances such as these, the bear always comes low and fast, sometimes without making any sounds, but other times with a grunt or a wuff. It would be necessary for us to bend over low to see under some spots. The bear was dark colored and would be difficult to see in the diminishing light. If either of us needed to get on our hands and knees to go through some of the densest thickets, we were to advise the other before beginning to crawl. I told Ron that I was not going to lift my scope covers as shooting, if it came to that, would be fast at extremely close range and barrel sighting would be all that time would allow. I told him to be careful and wished him good luck.

We began our slow, noisy journey down slope through the tangle of willows, dwarf birch, grass and blueberry growth. A single willow ptarmigan flushed close by me, which gave me a twitch, and a spike in my blood pressure, no doubt. Ron had a similar experience - buggered by a bird. We both heard single birds flush out downhill and ahead of us. We reckoned the bear had frightened the birds and focused on the area from which the noise came.

After about ten minutes of tense back and forth transecting, Ron was to my left when he yelled "BEAR" before shooting two times. The bear came busting through the brush toward me. I got a shot into the right front shoulder and another into the right ham as the bear continued past me and downhill. The bear's route was about fifteen yards from me. I paused to put two more bullets in my rifle.

We came together to compare notes. Ron said he saw the bear just off to his left side and about ten yards distant. As it came toward him he tried to brain shoot it, did hit it in the head and missed the second shot.

Ron moved to the right side of my position and we resumed our slow search. When I came to a ditch of about eight feet in depth and fifteen feet wide, I hollered to Ron that I was near the bank of a deep ditch and was uncomfortable with the situation. As I eased into the bottom of the ditch the bear immediately growled and wuffed three times, then rose up on the opposite side and turned toward me. I sighted down the barrel, aiming for the point of the jaw, but hit it in the neck, spinning it around. As it proceeded downhill, Ron hit it twice in the body.

Once more we reloaded our rifles. This time Ron had a good visual fix on where he last saw the bear and as we proceeded in that direction.

Again it got up on all fours and I put a bullet into the spine, rolling the bear. It stopped against a willow bush at the lower end of the thicket and thrashed a few seconds before going still. It was sudden death overtime for the Grizzly and I became aware of a sudden, profound silence.

Ron and I shook hands, reloaded our magazines and made sure the chambers were empty, then called to Brent to come.

Ron's first shot had blown out the upper and lower canine teeth and the cheek on the right side. My first shot broke the right humerus, the second entered the right ham, but hit no bones. My third shot struck the left side of the neck, missing the spine. Ron's third and forth shots were into the chest cavity and my last shot severed the spine just behind the front shoulder.

The dark Grizzly was a female with mature, developed nipples, but no sign of nursing cubs. Three days later, after fleshing, it squared nose to tail 7'3" and claw tip to claw tip 7'5", giving it a square measurement of 7'4". Its skull measured 21 12/16 inches. The silvertip hide was in ideal condition, being well furred and with no sign of rubbing.

Brent was ecstatic. He was full of wonder and praise at the conditions and outcome of this first day of his hunt. He said that he had been praying for us when we were in the brush after the wounded bear and was so relieved that we had found it and it had not injured either of us.

I suggested that it might be appropriate to now offer our thanks for the successful and dramatic conclusion of our endeavors. We three did that.

Light was fading fast, so after making photographs, we peeled the hide off, removed the hind quarters and the gall bladder to take back to camp and loaded Ron's pack board and mine for the walk back.

We arrived at the lodge an hour and a half later. I offered to make some super. As often happens at the end of a day like this, no one seemed especially hungry, so we snacked on smoked salmon with crackers and popcorn.

Lloyd had remained at the lodge and reported that two more groups of Caribou had come through using the same trail as the first herd of the day. Each mob had forty to fifty animals, but no outstanding bulls were among them.

We ended that day with a refreshing whiskey over ice.

September 3 opened with a temperature of plus twenty-nine, north wind of about ten miles per hours with occasional gusts to twenty-five in rain.

A band of approximately seventy-five Caribou came out of Break Ankle Canyon and traced the footsteps of the previous day's migrants. Before noon a herd of about three hundred animals came through. This group had a couple dozen mature bulls, one of which carried remarkably well palmated antlers. We four struck off as fast as we could boot up and go, but the animals were moving too fast for us.

Ron Phillips and Brent Wilson with Brent's big sow.

The rain continued, so we returned to the lodge and enjoyed mugs of hot coffee and snacks, when about 1:30 pm more Caribou came out of Break Ankle canyon and joined the others, making a mass of about five hundred animals scattered over the moguls at the mouth of East Bowl canyon. They were only from one quarter to three quarters of a mile from the lodge.

About six o'clock in the evening a band containing more than a dozen good bulls laid down near the cutback off the end of the runway. With the breeze at our back, we hustled to the base of the cut bank and eased our way toward the relaxed animals. When we rounded the last corner, the bulls were gone, so I took Brent up the cut bank and saw the bulls quartering away from us at about one hundred twenty yards distance. All the mature bulls were of similar antler quality, so to minimize the chance of picking the wrong one, I told Brent to shoot the last one in the string of animals.

His shot was high -because he held high - and I told him to just aim for what he wanted to hit and to squeeze the trigger lovingly - not jerk it!

The Caribou were now trotting away and disappeared in a small swale. I told Brent to hold for my instructions on which to shoot at...again.

When the string of animals emerged from the depression, none showed signs of having been hit, so I told Brent to take the big bull that was third from the end. This time the bull gave a bit of a lurch, followed by the distinctive "bung" sound of a gut shot. With the large group of animals now running, there was no opportunity for another clear shot. I shut down the video camera and visually followed the animals' movement toward the higher ground to the east. With my binoculars in use, I had a good fix on where the wounded bull was headed

I sent Ron and Lloyd back the way we'd come to hopefully head off the herd if they turned to the north. Brent and I moved into the swale and crouched down to watch and wait.

Within minutes another large band of Caribou came trotting in from the north. Upon sighting the new group of animals, the band with the wounded bull turned West to join them. As the two groups met they stopped and milled around. Though I scrutinized the milling mass of animals carefully, I could not pick out our cripple. I told Brent there would be no more shooting until we had that bull on the ground.

Some of the Caribou went back to feeding while others nervously glanced about for whatever had startled them. The group remained in the same location, so Brent and I approached them, bent over and walking slowly. I lifted the butt end of my rifle high over my head and moved it about, making no attempt to hide, hoping to appear like a feeding bull with a large antler. The Caribou were upwind from us. Their curiosity overcame them and they came toward us at a trot stopping a mere sixty yards off. A few cows began to move past us, then moved south to get our scent. Still, I could not spot the wounded bull. Once the downwind cows got our smell they snorted and turned, trotting off down creek. The biggest bunch of Caribou turned toward the eastern foothills. Finally I picked out the injured bull which was following a group of seven others, but as they gained elevation, he fell further and further behind. I told Brent that we must keep him in sight and I was confident that we could finish him off. As the string of bulls crested and topped over the skyline, the cripple began turning round and round and finally laid down in a spot we could easily keep in sight. He would soon be ours!

The coups de grace was delivered by Brent from forty yards. It was a good bull and especially good that it had not become the first wounded Caribou that I have ever lost.

As we took pictures and butchered the bull, with other Caribou streaming by, oblivious to our presence and activities.

As we returned to the lodge three mature bulls came on a path to intersect our own route. Brent had a second tag ready to use so we maneuvered to make that possible. At sixty yards, Brent shot his second bull of the day - and a good day it had been.

Everyone was back at the lodge just after eleven in the evening and ready for a meal. The pot of bear stew was delicious.

September 4 began with drizzle and +34 degrees, but with Caribou visible in all quadrants from the lodge windows everything was wonderful! All four of us searched the various herds for impressive racks.

It was a day to please the most picky of hunters. Patience and discrimination would surely be rewarded.

Lloyd had hunted with me several times in the past thirty years, taking two Grizzlies, two bull Moose and several Sitka Blacktail deer on Kodiak Island. His primary focus this time was a really big Caribou …. and a Wolf if the opportunity arose. Another Grizzly was a possibility, as he had a permit, but a bear was not high on his list this year.

After several hours of careful glassing from the main room of the lodge, locating potential targets with the binoculars, followed by closer examination with the "long eye" (my 15 to 60 power Bausch and Lomb spotting scope on a heavy tripod)…and hints of developing eyestrain, I found a bull that would tempt the most demanding of hunters. This animal wore antlers with nicely palmated uppers showing more than seven points on each side, outstanding bez with seven long tines - bilaterally, and well developed double shovels. In a group of about sixty animals which included several other eye catching bulls, he was clearly the greatest of the day. He might well turn out to be the best bull of the year. When you see an animal of this quality, long before all the tines are evaluated, you know it's a taker for sure.

The band he was with laid down and did not move for a couple of hours. They were resting in the middle of a large alluvial fan two miles Northwest of the lodge. Putting Lloyd within reasonable shooting range

Brent with his first Caribou trophy at the lodge.

would be a challenge. At 2:30 pm I sent Ron with Lloyd to stalk the big bull as I began to flesh Brent's Grizzly and Brent cut away meat from the skull.

After five hours of steady fleshing I had the bear skin ready for salting. On short breaks from his work on the skull, Brent had been keeping track of our friends from the window. We never heard the shot, but just before 8:00 pm we saw the big bull go down. The herd charged away down country toward the lodge.

Figuring it would take a couple of hours for the boys to return with the meat and trophy, I began to cook a big pot of spaghetti sauce.

About 10:00 pm Ron and Lloyd came in with that dandy bull and tired bodies.

We dined on the remainder of the bear stew, spaghetti, salad and fresh chocolate cake. It had been another productive, very good day - the third such in a row. The meat poles were laden with prime eating, hides were salted and our world was right.

September 5 dawned with a high overcast, a north wind of ten to fifteen miles per hour and a warmer + 42 degrees. As we were shoving breakfast down our necks a herd of approximately three hundred Caribou came out of East Bowl and turned south down Trail Creek. Seeing no remarkably good bulls in that bunch, we hiked up into the eastern foothills for better coverage of the valley.

The wind had grown tired, it seemed. In the calm, cool evening air we watched several short eared owls harvest lemmings from the swamp. A couple of snow shoe hares came close to the buildings to nibble at salt that had fallen from the hides.

A hearty dinner of barbequed caribou ribs, corn, salad and freshly baked cake put us all into a drowsy mood and we hit the racks early.

Gentle belches of the percolator brewing our coffee were the only sounds the next morning as our guests came up to see the heavy fog which hid even the outbuildings from our view.

Hints of break up of the nebulous cover began around ten and by noon the fog was lifting in spots. A slight southerly breeze cleared off the foothills and soon we were free of the damp obscuration.

Brent had been drawn for a Moose permit, so he and I headed down toward Popple Creek which often holds those giant deer this time of year. Ron and Lloyd hiked up creek to see what might be available.

We spotted twelve Caribou running across West Bowl fan with a bull in the lead. They were obviously spooked. Anytime I see a bull Moose or Caribou running in front of a band of cows in the fall time, I think… "Wolf"…and it usually proves to be the cause of this abnormal behavior. The Caribou dropped into the willows of Trail Creek and came toward us. Brent was wishing that he could take another one, but his legal limit had been reached. Brent told me he thought he heard a shot. Secretly I wondered if he was fantasizing. As the first Caribou came within two hundred yards of us, another group of forty with two very good bulls traced the same route.

Leaving Brent to continue glassing, I went back to the lodge to fillette a salmon for supper.

A light rain had set in, so I placed plastic tarps over the racks to protect our hanging winter meat. As I began to prepare the salmon, in came Ron and Lloyd with the first load of meat from a large Caribou. Brent had indeed heard a shot. After first spotting a white and a grey Wolf, the pair of hunters had seen the larger band of Caribou. It looked like the wolves had given up on the ungulates and headed north at a fast pace, so they maneuvered to get within range and Lloyd took his second big bull. This animal had a larger main beam, a massive body, and was good all around, but not quite so impressive as his first - but a taker, anytime.

As I prepared supper, Lloyd and Ron retrieved the rest of the meat, the cape and rack of his trophy.

After supper we took all took a much needed sauna, Ron & I did some personal laundry and we were ready to call it a day when my last survey with binoculars revealed a large Grizzly coming over three mile ridge toward the berry patch that had given us Brent's bear. It was too near dark for us to act on it, but I figured it would remain in the area, feeding on the rich berry patches.

We retired with the warm satisfaction of another good day and the possibility of Lloyd taking a Grizzly in the morning.

September 7 began with a soaker rain shower. We scrutinized Three

Lloyd with the beautiful bull Caribou.

Mile Ridge and all the berry patches between there and the lodge, as well as those well upstream, expecting to sight the big Grizzly, but he did not show. At one point someone hollered "Bear!" but it turned out to be a big porcupine. Those herbivores have a rolling stroll similar to that of a large bear and have fooled me countless times in the past. I once walked about three miles to check out one such "bear" that had ambled out of sight, only to discover a bristle pig.

Dall sheep had descended to feeding areas just above the willows. I guessed they had not scented Wolves recently and may be using this opportunity to savor some of the lower level delectables before freeze up.

Several dense flights of Willow Ptarmigan came down the valley and landed close to the lodge just before dark.

Color changes in the leaves of dwarf birch, blue berry bushes and cottonwood trees were remarkably advanced since the last time we noticed. Most years the leaves undergo an extreme color metamorphosis during the third week of August, which was delayed by more than two weeks this season, so it seemed the onset of winter may be delayed for this year.

As sunlight reached the valley on Saturday, September 8, with an outside temperature of plus twenty degrees, I watched frost form and grow in the clear, cold air. The newly generated frost would last for a couple of hours but was thick enough to provide tracking assistance until it melted away. Any tracks we saw in the frost would be freshly made. This was the first clear sky day I had seen since August 3. Morning sunlight hit the lodge at 11:45 am and soon dissolved the frost.

Ron and Lloyd walked north to glass some of the berry patches not visible from the lodge. Brent and I went south in hopes of locating a good bull moose for him. By mid afternoon we were at the rain swollen, icy East Bowl Creek. I looked around for a willow from which to cut walking sticks, but seeing none close by, I imprudently decided to go it without the aid of a third leg. Large boulders normally make secure stepping stones, but this year slick green moose covered most of them. As I was nearing the far side of the creek I slipped off a rock and plunged into a four foot deep hole, as I struggled to stand in the swift current and slippery rocks, I dowsed myself again. I was soaked and had submerged my rifle. Rats!

Brent from the other bank, offered to come to my assistance, but I told him to keep clear of the slick rocks and sloshed my way back to him.

Ashore, I sat on a tussock and removed my boots, then poured the water out and quickly put them back on, as I could feel my socks beginning to freeze in the cold air. I pointed out a high place from which to glass and told Brent to go there and glass for a couple of hours, making sure to return well before dark. If he saw a Moose with desirable antlers, he could shoot it, but only if it had at least four points on at least one of the brow shovels. There was no need for him to lose the chance of sighting his quarry.

As I hustled back I noticed some different looking lichens, so I pocketed samples for delivery to the National Park Service and the Alaska Department of Fish and Game. They could key them out and I would know what they were.

I set a brisk pace back to the lodge and was in the yard in less than an hour. Soaked or not, due to my exertion, I was not suffering much from the cold. I stripped off my clothes, wrung them out and hung them against the walls of the lodge and sauna building which felt warm to the touch in the afternoon sunlight. Before I got into dry shorts and under shirt, the chill had left me.

I disassembled the bolt of my Model 70, dried the rifle off with paper towels and oiled everything. This was not the first soaking for that fine old piece … or for me.

A small plane flew over and I recognized my friend Charles Dixon, who landed. I pulled on some britches and went to meet him. He accepted my invitation to stay the night with us.

I stoked up the sauna and began the supper of chicken fried Caribou, mashed potatoes and gravy, with salad and cranberry dessert.

Ron and Lloyd came in, having seen nine Caribou, but no bear. Brent reported seeing only Cairbou cows and calves.

The sauna felt good and we all hit our bags at 11:00 pm.

⚜

Sunday, September 9 dawned clear and cold at plus fifteen degrees. I had scheduled a trip to Kotzebue to deliver Lloyd and pick up our incoming hunter, David, but with such great hunting conditions and having seen the big Grizzly just two days before I decided to delay one day, so I called in an extension of my flight plan by 24 hours and called the incoming hunter to let him know the schedule. Brent was interested an a flight seeing excursion. Charles had agreed to take him, so off they went. Ron and Lloyd headed down creek to the South Overlook.

I used the day to fill my bear attracting plastic bottles with creosote. Hung around the buildings on a wire or string, bears can't resist biting them and since 1975, these attractants are probably why we have had no serious damage to the cabins by bears. I hang a couple dozen or more every year. Completing the bottling chore, I cut some willows from the runway and sawed up some dried wood for the sauna stove.

Upon their return, Brent and Charles reported seeing seven Caribou at the head of Trail Creek, while Ron and Lloyd spotted only one porcupine and some sheep.

For dinner we enjoyed baked chicken, macaroni and cheese, salad and fresh carrot cake.

⚜

Monday was our third day with visibility clear and unlimited. We loaded Charles airplane with about 400 pounds of meat. I took Lloyd with his antlers and gear and we departed about noon thirty. We flew directly on the GPS and landed in less than an hour and a half. It was a rush to get Lloyd's antlers crated for shipment, but he checked in and got on his jet. Someone had pilfered gas from my five hundred gallon tank, so I would need to get more at the bulk plant in the morning. David,

Lloyd and his second Caribou

the incoming hunter, was very patient and spent the night with me in the sod shack.

At the post office I ran into a friend who was planning to visit a buddy of mine in Nevada, so I handed him some prime Caribou backstraps to carry south.

Dropping the lichen samples off with both the Federal and State offices, I later learned that one was a "transient lichen", which grows on the surface without roots - in forty-five years, I had never noticed one before. The other was a spore bearing lichen, also new to me.

David and I departed Kotzebue for the lodge about 4:00 pm. The flight was pleasant with no turbulence and we saw about sixty sheep.

After sighting in David's rifle and making a shot with mine, we dined on chili and hit the hay after midnight.

Wednesday, September 12 began with a high overcast and +22 degrees. Ron and Brent went down creek to fish while I took David to the East Moguls to glass for whatever we might see. We saw only sheep. Brent caught both Arctic Char and Grayling.

About 3:00 pm a Cessna 206 landed and two men got out. It was a local charter plane and I later learned that a State Fish and Game inspector had come to check licenses, etc. We watched them from our glassing position. They missed us this time, but there was nothing amiss, anyway.

Dinner this time was pressure cooked, barbequed Caribou ribs, potatoes and fresh chocolate cake.

The next day, after bacon, biscuits and gravy, Ron and Brent walked to the South Overlook for Moose or Wolves, but saw only sheep.

David and I went north and half a mile from the lodge encountered eleven Caribou. The only bull in the bunch was a young one and I encouraged David to hold his fire in expectation of a better trophy. We walked on past the Bear Stairs and glassed for two hours in a chilly north wind. The same band of Caribou walked just below us, heading north. Had I to do it over, I would have let David shoot one of the bulls, but this was not the first time I had a hunter hold off, only to not get another opportunity.

Snowshoe hares had been on a rapid population increase from 2005 through 2011, but this year they were in short supply. Frequent Lynx sign and the one sighting we made in the yard probably explained the hare shortage. Over predation normally is followed by a decrease in the local carnivore numbers and a rebound of hares. I hope we see that take place in this cycle. We spotted only three hares this day.

Brent had remained past the normal twelve day booking in hopes of taking a Moose. He had been with us in 2011 when a world class bull walked by the lodge on September 15, but this year, Moose sign was scarce and we had not seen a single one. He decided he would just go home on September 14. I didn't argue the point, but did mention that another day or two might pay off. It was a long shot, of course.

Saturday, September 14 began as another calm, clear, cold day. The thermometer indicated +18 degrees. We enjoyed a good breakfast of scrambled eggs and salmon hash, glassed from the lodge, loaded the cub and departed about 1:00 pm. I took a short sashay up Trail Creek, but saw only sheep. We turned south, popped over the ridge to the Kuguroruk

River and after crossing the Noatak River we flew down the Miumerak Creek. The locals refer to a couple of mountain lakes that I used to camp on as "Jake's Lakes". They were calm and beautiful this crisp fall day. Sheep were out in large numbers and feeding low on the slopes, but we saw no Moose or Caribou.

After getting Brent confirmed for his early morning departure and purchasing three large fish shipping containers, I did some grocery shopping before heading to the shack. We took our dinner at the hospital restaurant and returned to crate his antlers and pack his hides and meat. We were tucked into our beds before ten o'clock.

As we got Brent checked in for the Alaska Airlines flight the next morning at 6:30am, the terminal was loaded with hunters in new camouflage outfits. None but Brent had any meat or trophies to check in. As we waited for the jet to arrive, several fellows came to ask us where we had found the animals, as they had seen none. I passed out several of my business cards, but most of these Americans would not consider a fully guided hunt, opting for a seemingly less expensive "drop-off" Transported services.

Most of the Transporter trips wind up costing the guest hunters more money for five to seven days of hunting from a tent than I charge for a twelve day guided trip from the lodge, and success rates for the high volume operations are only about fifteen percent. But the people think they're getting it on the cheap. Oh well.

It seems there's plenty of things to do in Kotzebue and I am always glad to climb back in the cub and get out of town.

A dark, ragged overcast had moved in making my trip north turbulent and wet as I flew through several big rain and snow squalls, but Trail Creek was nearly calm and dry.

It was time to change the oil in the airplane, so I took advantage of the nice conditions and the warm engine to drain out the old lubricant for use in the sauna stove and set seven quarts of new oil in the lodge for putting in warm whenever I decided to fly again. As I finished up at the airplane a large bull Moose came strolling up the runway making his plosive grunts as he walked. He was looking for love and oblivious to me and the aircraft. Oh man, I wished that Brent had remained for this. He would have been ecstatic at an opportunity for such a beast and we would have had nearly no meat packing to do, as well as an abundance of fine eating for the coming winter. Murphy rides with us all and I'm sure ole Murph was giggling at me…and Brent.

Sunday, September 16 came with clear skies, plus twenty degrees and a north wind of fifteen to twenty miles per hour. North of us the heavy overcast was depositing snow and by mid afternoon, visibility was reduced to a quarter of a mile and snow covered everything. Late in the day we saw another bull moose walked up the strip and passed within ten yards of the airplane. That was rubbing it in, for sure. As we got ready to retire a hard rain noisily pelted the roof.

Monday broke with a four thousand foot overcast, plus thirty degrees and a light north wind. Most of the snow was gone from the valley floor, but it remained at five hundred feet and above. By noon we were getting a south wind at fifteen to twenty miles per hour with drizzle and fog.

David took a three hour nap after lunch. Ron and I puttered around with preparations for closing the lodge for winter. I cooked up a batch of spaghetti and after some stories and reading we all went to bed.

The south wind remained steady into the next morning and brought a new cover of snow. We three walked up to the East Moguls to glass for about three hours but saw only sheep and a couple large flocks of ptarmigan. We were back in the lodge by 7:00 pm for baked chicken, vegetables and cake.

Wednesday revealed a new layer of snow, followed by a steady rain throughout the rest of the day. We enjoyed the comforts of the lodge and made use of the library. We were all thankful to not be out on a flooding gravel bar in a tent.

Thursday, September 21 we awoke to thick fog, making it impossible to see the sauna building fifty yards from the lodge. Shortly after noon, as the fog began to lift, we climbed again to the East Moguls to look for game, but nothing was moving it seemed. This was a damp and chilly day with no encouragement from the animals so we went back to the lodge at 5:00 pm. The broadcast radio said heavy rains were causing sever flooding in the Delta, Susitna, Talkeetna and Matanuska rivers. Some bridges were washed out.

The local radio reported that a resident of Kiana had shot my friend and aircraft mechanic, Paul Buckle and his brother in their tent camp on the Squirrel River. The shooter used Paul's .44 magnum pistol, hitting both men in the chest, then fled down the river in their boat, leaving them for dead. The next day, Paul was able to get a radio distress call out and the badly wounded men were picked up and flown to Kotzebue. The shooter was still on the loose.

Friday morning the dense fog was back, but it began to lift by 9:00 am. I spotted a large grey wolf on the west alluvial fan. It appeared to be searching for rodents. I suggested to David that we try to get within range for a shot, but he was more interested in not missing his jet flight home, so we departed about noon. I told Ron he was free to try to take that wolf, if he wanted to do so, as soon as we departed.

Fog was still patchy - heavy in places - and was dense at the squeeze spot on Trail Creek west of Misheguk Mountain. I lowered flaps and proceeded down stream with reasonable vertical visibility, then broke out after about two miles. At the mouth of Trail Creek we spotted three large bull Muskoxen being stalked by a huge Grizzly. The bovines were aware of the bear and had their rumps together. That bear would have been a dandy to collect. Fog was still patchy thick, so I flew through the Noatak flats to town.

After getting David squared away in a local bed and breakfast I went back up for Ron. Rain, snow and fog still had the direct route socked in so I went through the flats again. I didn't take time to look for the large Grizzly near the three muskoxen.

Ron had lost sight of the wolf shortly after we left, so he went about getting the place ready to close up. We were soon back in the air. With no meat or hides to haul, the cub was quickly off the ground.

This time the lower Trail Creek was more open and we saw seven large bull Muskoxen all bunched up with a medium sized Toklat Grizzly on one side and a cream colored bear on the other. This was only about six miles from the lodge - a shame it had not taken place closer to the lodge. We landed on runway 18 in Kotzebue just at dark.

After grabbing a burger to go, we unloaded our gear and went to Paul Buckle's house to hear the latest on that issue. Several guides and Transporters had gathered and the whiskey was flowing. Paul's brother was in worse shape, but both had been flown to an Anchorage hospital and full recovery was expected for each of them. The mood was extremely angry and some mentioned lynching the shooter who had been apprehended and was in the local jail. I figured it was time for Ron and I to go home.

Saturday the twenty-second opened nice in Kotzebue. For several years I'd been planning to take Ron up to the Wullik River for some fresh sea-run Arctic Char. Normally the big, fat trout are stacked up like cord wood in the holes and strike voraciously at artificial lures or flies. The night before, the aviation outlook forecast was for strong winds north of town, so after hearing that Kivalina was blowing NE 30, gusting to 40, we drove down to the Flight Service station, where we learned that the report was correct. It was already turbulent and promised to get much worse. So, once again, our fishing trip would have to be cancelled.

A Transporter friend called to say he had a bunch of Caribou meat to distribute. We stopped by, most of what remained was badly bloodshot, but we took it and dropped it off to some elderly people who appreciated it.

As Ron secured his stand-by seat on the evening Alaska Airlines jet, I drained about 60 gallons of fuel out of my big tank into small containers to be stored in the vans. Left in the large tank, it would likely disappear over the winter and I've never liked the idea of providing fuel for thieves.

After Ron's departure I did some paperwork for ADF&G on licenses and tag sales, then hit the sack. The wind had picked up to about 30 mph and was quite noisy.

Sunday morning, after checking the airplane, I drove down to the Episcopal Church to hear my old friend Wilfred Lane deliver his sermon. Wilfred is as fine an example of a true Christian as I have known. He has had several bouts with brain cancer and showed serious surgical scars on his head. He had been ill again this summer and most people expected him to meet his maker soon. As I walked in at the ringing of the bell, Wilfred was at the door, took my hand and said "Jake, we've been waiting for you."

"I'm sorry to be late, my friend."

Wilfred smiled as he said "Jake, it's never too late, my friend."

There were only six people in attendance, which has become the norm, unfortunately. This morning's sermon was about baptism and at the conclusion, Wilfred asked, "Jake, are you ready?" With no hesitation, I said, "Yes, I am ready."

What a moving experience! Wilfred said this might prove to be his last baptism and he was so happy that it was me. But he added that it was all in God's hands.

We enjoyed some cookies and coffee after the ceremony and I drove Wilfred and his wife, Vivian home.

Normally I would have switched from my Borer (high performance) prop to my cruise prop, but it was windy and cold and looked like I may be stuck in Kotzebue for several days, so I got organized for closing up the shack and departing when conditions permitted.

The old '77 ford pickup quit, due to a solenoid short, which ate up a couple hours that chilly afternoon, but with the help of my friend, John Rae, I got it running.

Monday passed quickly with local chores, mailing in payments to various places and some visiting. The four o'clock forecast indicated I might be able to get to Fairbanks the next day, Tuesday, which would be nice.

Tuesday came with plus thirty degrees, calm conditions and a skiff of new snow, as well as an extremely adherent layer of frost coating the plane. I broomed and roped off the wings and control surfaces several times, then decided I should turn the cub to pick up the sunlight to clear the frost. Removing the frost took over two hours, but I took off at 11:15 am. I was able to climb to 9,500 feet where the outside air temperature was +18 degrees, beneath a high, dark overcast to the east. I was comfortably dressed and the heater made it a pleasant flight. From Kobuk Lake I could see Purcell Mountain, and once there, the Hogatza Range and Indian Mountain were visible. The visibility remained remarkably good all the way to Chena Marina, where I landed at 4:45 pm. Headwinds had slowed me down by as much as 20 mph in places, but five and a half hours for that 440 mile trip is not bad. My airspeed indicated 92-95 mph, but ground speed averaged only 80 mph. I drained the hot oil and unloaded the cub.

I picked up my eighteen year old daughter Bess at her University of Alaska dorm and we enjoyed a Mexican dinner and a good visit.

Wednesday was active with getting pickling oil and running the engine for fifteen minutes to soak everything with the preservative. I ran a quick check on compression and all cylinders were good. A quick shower at the Fairbanks International Airport pilot lounge - a wonderful facility which would be welcome in every airport, and a haircut had me ready for dinner again with Bess.

The next day I drove the truck to spend two days in Anchorage before driving down to Homer to catch the ferry to Kodiak. It had been an imperfect, but good season.

Most Remote

The best years of my youth - those that left me with the best memories - were the ones when my family and I lived in remote places. I never minded having fewer kids to hang around with, or "hang out" as today's kids term it.

We lived at a remote mine in Southern Arizona, making a 30 mile bus ride to and from school every day. There was another kid, about 4 years older than me at the site and we enjoyed each other's company most of the time, as we caught feral burros, burned out anthills, practiced pole vaulting and hunted everything from bugs to deer after our domestic survival chores, like tending the garden and maintaining the dirt road, were done.

On the ranch in Montana, where I spent summers with my uncle, Stan, there were no other teenagers around, just men, working hard, seven days a week. I loved it, every bit of it. And, work load permitting, I got to do a little fishing and varmint hunting some evenings.

School required that I spend two years at the University of Arizona in Tucson, where I fully engaged myself in getting most of a Bachelor of Science in Biology requirements done in two years. My goal was to be accepted to a good Dental School, get through that training, and move to a remote little town in British Columbia or Alaska.

Following four years of living in Portland, Oregon during Dental School, I was assigned to the Marine Hospital on the East Coast, spending most of my time in Baltimore, with periods in Cape May, New Jersey, Washington, D.C. and other overly urbanized areas. But my dream of the far North carried me through. I kept a large map of Alaska on my living room wall.

By great good fortune I was transferred to the Indian Health Service and although it was based in Alaska's largest city, Anchorage, or "Anguish" as I called it, I traveled throughout rural, remote Alaska for two years. After my first trip there, I knew that I would settle eventually in Kotzebue which is about as remote a town as one can find.

Further amazingly good fortune led me, quite by happenstance, to Trail Creek in 1968. In the 1970s my wife, Mae, and I proved up on an 80 acre allotment located 118 GPS miles north of Kotzebue, The Bureau of Land Management surveyors told me when they did their assessment and survey at our site, that it was the most remote privately owned property in the United States. That suited me just fine. I liked the thought of it - even more, I liked the location.

A recurring nightmare for me since the early 1970s is that of a school bus coming up the creek. Another frequent bad dream is that some mining operation suddenly appears up creek from me, destroying the pristine beauty and calm of the entire valley. Hopefully neither horror will ever come true.

With the National Park Service having control of the Noatak National Preserve within which our acreage sits, close proximity of new neighbors is unlikely, but I am very aware of the fact that government can do whatever it wants to do, when ever it wants to, and it will do it legally. For now, at least, we are insulated from a rush of new neighbors.

⌣⌣⌣,⌣⌣⌣

Initially we set up a large wall tent which accommodated our needs adequately. When I began booking hunting guests, additional sleeping tents became necessary. Each year during our absence, the main tent frame was chewed to pieces by Grizzly bears. I began to be concerned about a bear attack on us or our guests while in a tent, so in 1973 I pre-assembled a 12 foot by 12 foot cabin and flew it up to Trail Creek in one trip with the Civil Air Patrol Beaver supplemented with several trips in my Cessna 180 and my Piper Super Cub.

As soon as the aufis glacier receded enough to use the strip, I took Mae, our daughter Sandy and my sister Pat up to help put the cabin together. We had it up with the plywood roof in place the first day, and for the first time in the history of the world, humans slept inside a solid structure on Trail

Creek. That tiny cabin was a Godsend, after using tents for several years.

We still put some guests up in a wall tent with a wood stove in it, as they seemed to prefer "roughing it" to that extent, but as things got cooler each fall, the solid walls and insulated roof of the little shack seemed to hold the heat better than any tent. I began planning for more cabin space.

The original 12' x 12' cabin - 1973.

Later, in August, a bit more than a month after we built the small cabin, a blond Grizzly put Mae and our daughter Sandy on the roof of the cabin, where I saw them when I came in with a load of materials in the Cessna 180. Had the cabin not been there, I believe Mae would have killed the bear, but it was good that had not been necessary.

Just 14 months after we put the cabin up, Mae and I were sleeping one September morning when a female Toklat Grizzly broke a window, tore off one wall panel and had partially entered the cabin with us before I shot it. There might well have been a mauling or worse, if not for the 3/8 inch plywood walls. The next summer I added an extra half inch course of plywood to the exterior walls.

Our next project was a 12 foot by 8 foot two story addition to the little shack. This allowed 2 or 3 guests to accompany Mae and I inside solid walls and allowed me, at least, to sleep better when we had guests in camp. Actually, I think everyone slept more peacefully.

We were spending more and more time at Trail Creek and decided to build a proper lodge in 1979. I drew the plans on graph paper, figured the materials and ordered most of what we needed from Seattle. The barge was delayed, so it was late September before we had time to arrange for a chartered DeHaviland Otter to make three trips to the camp with building materials, and I had two Honda 110 ATC three wheelers flown up on top of the lumber, as well.

Putting on the first addition. Note the Willow growth.

Lodge at Trail Creek, 2009

We got the ATCs and most of the materials stored and weather proofed on the nearby site we had selected for the lodge. The fellow helping me, Ray, had mentioned that he could build a bear proof enclosure for the insulation, but I said he should not even try, rather he should just stuff it all into the existing cabin. When I came back with the last load, he had done it his way. I was disgusted but weather and time did not allow us to tear his boxing apart and put the batts of fiberglas insulation inside. I was sure the bears would do that for us.

Sure enough, the following April, a bear tore into the "bear proof" box and after shredding it, scattered all the insulation. I was not happy about that and nearly did not retain Ray to help with the construction of the lodge, but decided to keep him on. I have always been glad that I kept him, as he was the best bush carpenter and "make do" guy that I have ever come across. And he was always pleasant company, to boot. He and I had the two story lodge up in less than five weeks of long hours in spite of the most horrendous mosquito harassment either of us had ever endured. That building has withstood the ravages of Arctic storms and bear assaults for over thirty years.

Passive solar heating keeps the upstairs comfortable without supplementary heat from the oil stove in all but the coldest fall weather. We paid careful attention to moisture barriers and tight insulation and the lodge is about as snug as possible.

To a man, and especially women, our guests have all remarked about the quality of the accommodations we provide in such a remote, often hostile environment. We have enjoyed the location and the buildings far beyond our initial expectations.

Several Grizzly bears have been shot from the windows of the lodge, some of which had threatened our safety.

In 1981 I flew up one single engine Otter load of materials and put together a shop to house the Hondas, to flesh skins during inclement weather and added a sauna at the back. Saunas are far and away the most effective and pleasant way for a gang of people to keep clean and comfortable in a remote situation. The sauna room also serves as a drying facility for cloths and boots, and is much appreciated by all.

Finally, after using Coleman lanterns for so many years, in 2009, I put in a solar panel and installed electric lights in every room of the lodge.

Changes on Trail Creek

Some aspects of the area are changing. In the 1960s through the late 1980s we had winter ice for our use throughout the fall. Trail Creek is a braided stream and the channels freeze to the bottom in early winter, but the force of springs and surface drainage puts flowing water up over the top of the ice, which then also freezes, building up layers of hard ice. This formation is called an aufis (pronounced "off ice") glacier. At times the ice near the landing strip has been over ten feet thick. Like all glacier ice, it is more dense and holds its coldness longer than commercial freezer ice. It is nice in cocktails, as well.

However, since the mid 1990s, we have needed to fly ice in for kitchen use and keeping our perishables.

Keeping the new willows cut back on the landing strip has become a tedious chore in the past several years. Without our annual cutting and removal of new brush, we would soon have no place to land the aircraft.

The Wolf population has increased over the years and an active den is located about 4.2 GPS miles down the creek from the lodge. It has been used annually for over forty years. Wolf sightings during the summer have become common. I believe the elimination of Wolf hunting from aircraft during the winter, along with a huge increase in the Barren Ground Caribou numbers have been the primary causes of the currently over abundant Wolf population.

Alaska/Yukon Moose moved into Trail Creek valley in the early 1970s and peaked after twenty years. Since the early 1990s, Moose numbers have dropped precipitously. We observe huge, world class bulls every year as they move up and down Trail Creek valley in search of mating partners, but not in nearly the numbers we saw two decades ago. In the late 1970s, between 80 and 90 adult Moose over wintered on Trail Creek. By 2005, about 20 Moose called Trail Creek home. Fortunately the local Moose were seeded with powerful genetic potential and the area bulls grow large, well palmated antlers. The exuberant willows of several species provide superb nutrition. If the bulls are allowed to attain five to seven years of age, they usually have tremendous headgear. There have been two periods of eight straight years when I observed no calves on my flights between Kotzebue and the lodge. In 2010, nearly all cows were accompanied by at least one calf. I believe the near total absence of Wolves in the area that year resulted in the Moose calf survival.

Caribou rarely over winter in the area around the lodge, but in 2005 and 2006 we found fresh shed antlers, indicating that Caribou had been present until the end of November. Most years, between July 1 and July 15, a huge post calving aggregational movement of Caribou comes up Trail Creek, leaving some small groups and individual stragglers that remain throughout the summer. By mid to late August, we see bands of Caribou moving southward. In 2008 and 2009, every Caribou we saw was headed North throughout August and September. In 2010, we saw only seven Caribou on Trail Creek, four of which were abandoned calves. The main herd of Caribou remained on the North Slope that year, finally moving South beginning in late September and continuing sporadically through the end of November. Most of the animals that did eventually depart the North Slope exited by passes far to the East of their more commonly used routes.

The Dall sheep population on Trail Creek seemed to drop a bit in the early 1990s, but in 2010, I observed more sheep from the lodge windows than ever before, counting 65 rams and over 200 sheep total. Wolves, and to a much lesser extent, Golden Eagles are the main predators of sheep. In 2009 we found the remains of seven mature rams killed by Wolves. We found where one group of four rams had apparently been caught in deep snow in a narrow canyon just east of the lodge. Three of the seven sheep had been big rams of ten years age or older.

Musk Oxen, reintroduced to the Arctic in the 1970s have proliferated and since 1988 we have seen single bulls on Trail Creek annually. I had never seen a cow or calf group of Musk Oxen in the vicinity of the lodge until 2011 when a group of five cows and four calves appeared about five miles downstream from the lodge.

Grizzly bears have increased over the past forty years. Trail Creek in the 1970s was host to many sows and cubs, but males became the main cohort by the early 1980s.

The last Black Bear observation that I made on Trail Creek took place in 1978. I believe the Grizzlies have killed and driven off the smaller species of bears in the western Brooks Range.

Snowshoe Hares peaked in 1980, but that April, I found many scats showed bloody diarrhea and did not see a hare again until 2005. By 2008, we commonly observed several hares from the lodge windows at dusk. I noticed small, strange looking craters around the buildings, then saw hares digging and eating the dirt at the edges of the holes. Any place where we had laid out a salted skin attracted the hares, which ate the dirt for the sodium chloride residue from the salted skins.

The much larger Arctic Hares occasionally are found on Trail Creek, but only rarely do they appear in that area.

Red Fox and Arctic Fox are seen much more frequently when the Hare population is abundant.

Canadian Lynx are rare on Trail Creek, but we observed a large male in the yard of the lodge on several occasions in 2010 and found lynx tracks in 2011. In 2012 we saw a large Lynx just outside the lodge door, but that summer the hare population was much reduced. I suspect the Lynx were responsible for the drop in the hare numbers.

Willow Ptarmigan inhabit the area, but that species had a low period in their population cycle from 1998 through 2005. In addition to local birds, large flocks, sometimes numbering in the thousands, pass through during September and October as they migrate off the North Slope.

In 1978, Mae and I shot three Spruce Grouse out of a flock of ten birds near the lodge.

Trail Creek is a spawning area for Arctic Char and Dolly Varden and their numbers have remained relatively constant over the 45 years that I have spent on the creek.

Grayling are residents of the creek and they remain throughout the year. Small sculpin are found occasionally.

In 1980 I hooked and landed an eight pound "jack" King salmon. In 1978 I observed a few Pink salmon on the lower end of Trail Creek.

So, as they say, times change.

The Wife's Revenge

Over the years I've lost more than one booked hunter due to spousal pressures from their "better half". In my view those better halves were not so - not better, I mean,...but that determination is far too complex to quantitate here.

Lots of the fellows are busy keeping up with the demands of their work, sometimes leading them to ask their wife to pack their bags for their hunting trip to Alaska. That seems reasonable to me - if you trust your wife and if she hasn't been pressing for new carpeting, cookware or jewelry with the money you plan to spend on the hunting trip.

Some guests were immediately and openly vocal about their victimization by their spouse, others tried to keep it secret. One recurring trick employed by irritated wives seems to be to pack their panties (this couldn't be accidental... could it?) rather than the man's under shorts, for the poor fellow to wear among his hairy chested hunting buddies. That's really thoughtful - cunning may be a more appropriate term - sending hubby off on a hunting trip with a gang of men, some of whom may be friends, but some will likely be strangers. I view such acts as no more than humorous mischief. Some men consider such a premeditated act to be an especially cruel manifestation of female depravity.

I have a remedy for such occurrences. It is my automatic, infallible, washing machine - a scrub board and large tub. As guest hunters all arrive (I assume) wearing a pair of shorts, they could use my scrub board to wash them out, then hang them in the sauna to dry. Some fellows happily use my equipment to clean their lone pair of skivvies, but most just relented and wore the wife's panties. These ill considered acquiescenses led to some humorous verbal exchanges between our guests, particularly when the initiate cross dresser tried to get by without being noticed. Our sleeping rooms accommodate two or three guests - one can easily imagine the consternation of relative strangers when the new room mate comes in, prepares to crawl into his sleeping bag, and slips out of his long pants to reveal a feminine set of undies. When the britches come down, eyebrows - and suspicions, are raised.

Wives seem to choose the most outlandish ladies unmentionables to send along on hunting trips. I never would have dreamed that such remarkably salacious under garb existed, had I not been there to witness it. But in my rural existence, I've been sheltered, I guess.

Early one morning, years ago, as I came by the wash basin, I noticed that someone's panties were in a wad and had been cast into the garbage. They were not soiled, so I hoisted that particularly eye catching pair of frilly dilly knickers on the pole just beneath the windsock before our guests awakened. That pole attracts everyone's attention as it's message dictates which direction we will hunt and other useful information. Sure enough, before much coffee had been swallowed, someone made note of the lingerie, waving gaily in the breeze. No one claimed the knickers, so I left them hanging. The unrelenting winds soon had those delicate undergarments in tatters, which led to some interesting conjecture regarding how such intimate apparel might become so shredded, especially if adorning the loins of the person who had planted them for their unsuspecting spouse. Good taste dictates that I do not detail that imaginative conversation here.

One extraordinarily alert guest of mine discovered this base treachery on his first night in the north, as he prepared to shower in the Kotzebue hotel. The following morning he asked that he be allowed a quick trip to the general store for something important. I dropped him by the general store and went inside with him. When he found no men's shorts on the shelf, he asked if there might be some available, but there were none. In sheer desperation he bought a couple large (they were circus sized) pairs of solid color women's panties. At first I was confused and somewhat concerned at his choice of underwear, - that was until I saw the especially colorful, daintily adorned bloomers his wife had packed for him, then I clearly understood his choice and motivation. Score one for the wife.

Newly discovered panties flutter beneath the wind sock.

Hunters, take warning! If you don't pack your own bags, be certain that you inspect them for all the vital items you may need, including a change or two of skivvies or be prepared to suffer the sometimes ignominious consequences mentioned herein.

It's disconcerting to sort through one's luggage for the usual Fruit of the Loom and come up with eye candy.

Why I Like the Winchester Model 70

Just about everybody has a favorite gun or rifle. I've seen some pretty fancy, extraordinarily expensive firearms that are touted to be "the best" because of this or that characteristic, but I've always preferred factory models - made by United States gun makers, - and reasonably priced.

The Winchester Model 70 has always been popular, especially the pre-64 models. Within a month of my arrival in Alaska, in 1967, I had a part time job as an Assistant Guide working for a Registered Guide who used a Model 70 chambered for .300 Winchester magnum. That caliber had more umph than my 30:06, the biggest gun I had, but I reasoned that with his experience as a recommendation, I should purchase a similar rifle. Using the same ammunition as another in the hunting party could be potentially invaluable.

One weekend during the fall of 1967, I saw a nearly new Winchester Model 70 in .300 WnMag for sale in the Anchorage paper. It was manufactured that same year, so it missed the mark of the ultimate pre-64 rifles, but for $70 I thought it was a good buy. The stock was a cheap piece of wood, softer than most stocks, but the rifle shot accurately.

An elderly hunter with wide experience had told me that if a barrel was one of the first produced using a new tap, it's chances for being consistently accurate were improved. If that is the case, my rifle barrel may have been the very first cut from a new tap.

By experiment I learned that the pre-64s would jack rounds in from an upside down position more effectively than the later model 70s, but I doubted that I would be using it upside down much, if ever. So far, for the past 47 years I have always been right side up when shoving a round into the chamber.

The bluing wore off parts of the barrel on the first long trip. But that didn't bother me at all.

That rifle shot well in my hands and in the hands of others, to whom I have frequently found it necessary to hand my weapon.

After about ten years of using that rifle, a guest hunter that I will call Hank, and I were in pursuit of a dandy Grizzly downstream from the lodge. The bear was cruising through the brush and trees along Trail Creek, stopping to clear the snow and dig out roots of Eskimo potatoes, or "masu", as it ambled along, browsing on berries and keeping to the cover.

The wind was helpfully consistent as we tried to maneuver to give us a clear view of the bruin. I kept hoping he would find something to hold his attention - and his body - long enough for us to get set up for a shot.

After more than two hours of weaving around we saw the bear turn onto an open gravel bar. It walked spread legged across the ice on the river, clawed it's way to the top of a cut bank and disappeared into the Dwarf Birch "pucker brush" beyond.

We paused, hoping to avoid being seen or heard by the bear, then began to cautiously slide our boots across the smooth ice. Mindful of the possible opportunity for a shot before we completed the crossing, I had the guest hunter in front, with me about 6 feet behind him.

When walking with a rifle, I normally use the butt of the gun as a third leg for stability, especially in slippery situations. I suggested to Hank that he do that also as we crossed the slick ice.

Hank weighed about 240 pounds. The bear was probably in the neighborhood of three times that, but had the weight more effectively distributed with its wider spaced, broader feet - and it had four of 'em.

Midway across the river, the ice cover abruptly gave way, dropping Hank into a waist deep hole. I tried to back up, but ended up on my butt in icy water over my hip boots and nearly to my navel. Both our rifles were soaked in the rapidly freezing water. Somehow, luckily, neither of us had shouted. The bear was likely unaware of our position or condition.

I grabbed the collar of Hank's coat and, as I broke through the ice separating us from the shore, I drug him, spewing and gasping, back to where we'd started to cross.

Hank had a Remington with some spendy after factory modifications, but the action was original. In the cold air, both our soaked actions froze up. I immediately forced mine open and removed the bolt, and told him to do the same. I thrust my bolt inside my jacket and under my left armpit to warm it. Hank did likewise. Those icy bolts were a cruel torture under our arms, but it seemed the only reasonable solution to our dilemma. We were both soaked through and feeling the biting cold.

My rifle muzzle was covered by electrician's tape, which I removed to be able to look into the tube to make sure that the barrel was free of ice, which it was. Next, I inspected Hank's barrel. It too, was free of obstructions.

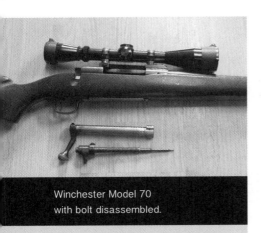

Winchester Model 70 with bolt disassembled.

This piece appeared in the 2013 Winter Convention issue of THE ALASKA PROFESSIONAL HUNTER - but the text following "take that fine, old bear." was omitted and the lower photo showed only the rifle with the bolt out, not the disassembled bolt pieces. Two serious compromises made inadvertently by the editor.

After a few minutes, I put my bolt back in the action and set it on half safety before removing it again and unscrewing the firing pin/main spring assembly from the bolt's interior, from which I blew off the traces of water, then put both pieces back under my armpit for more warming prior to wiping it off with my still dry shirt sleeve. The icy pieces of steel felt like hot pokers on my bare skin.

Hank had no experience in disassembling a Remington bolt, which is not easy to do in the field, but by keeping his bolt in his armpit, hopefully the firing pin would remain functional. He shook the bolt off in an attempt to remove any water that had entered its interior.

I dried my two bolt pieces on my sleeve, reassembled the bolt and dry fired it. It functioned normally.

Hank wondered if we should continue, but this was a good bear and I wanted to at least have a look over the cutbank.

Given the circumstances, we needed to keep moving or the cold would soon make us really miserable, so why not go the little bit further, I reasoned?

We went down stream to a braided area with open, shallow riffles and crossed, then eased our way along the cut bank, rifles ready, but nothing in the chamber.

Then, there was the bear periodically showing his back, about a hundred and fifty yards into the knee high brush. He was head down and busily occupied feeding on something. We were downwind and crept to within 80 yards before I told Hank to chamber a round. I chambered too, with no difficulty.

Hank got a shell up the spout and we crept to within about 60 yards. I told Hank to shoot when he got a clear shot and was ready. But when he squeezed the trigger there was only a faint click. Enough ice was inside his bolt to prevent the mainspring from igniting the primer.

The bear looked up, but not our way. I silently handed Hank my rifle, with a round chambered and ready, and I whispered to him to aim for what he wanted to hit. Our motion alerted the bear which turned, then stood up to get a better view. Hank aimed for the middle of the chest and his shot was true. The bear dropped to all fours and ran away from us, but I saw him go straight into a thick cluster of brush and pile up. I was sure we had him. The bear acted like it was heart shot.

I fussed a little with Hank's bolt but could not get it to dry fire, so I lit a cigar to slow us down - a contemplative period with a cigar is so often time well spent. That day our wet, cold situation hastened this ritual a bit.

I checked my rifle by dry firing it again and after about five minutes, - me with my own rifle in hand and Hank carrying his disabled weapon - we approached the dark form lying in the spot where I'd last seen the bear.

Indeed, it was the big boar, and it was stone dead, with its eyes wide open in a vacant stare.

Had I been using any rifle other than a Model 70, we would not have continued after getting so wet, nor would we have had an opportunity to take that fine, old bear.

We were about three and a half miles downstream from the lodge and thoroughly soaked, which caused us considerable discomfort while skinning the big bear. Our pants had stiffened as ice formed on the outside.

Jake sitting aboard the big boar Grizzly.

After I got a willow fire going we took off our hip boots, wrung out our socks and flapped our arms like a pair of excited geese as we worked to generate body warmth. It was no fun pulling those wet, cold hip boots back on! A few dozen pushups revved up our circulatory systems and sent warmer blood coursing through our bodies. It helped.

And, as we skinned it, the bear's body warmth felt good on our painfully cold hands.

As soon as we began packing the hide and hind quarters back to the lodge, the physical exertion coupled with the satisfaction of bagging that record sized critter was further enhanced by the expectation of a warm meal, followed by a little snort and comfortable beds, warmed us up to a more tolerable state.

Hot chocolate laced with Peppermint Schnapps after a quickly heated supper of canned chili and pilot bread, hit the spot. We hung our wet britches, gloves and sox up near the wood stove and dozed off, thankful for that memorable day which ended with the warm shelter and sleeping bags.

The following day I browned some small pieces of bear meat, adding some potatoes, carrots, onions and beef bouillon to make a stew as I went about removing the skull and paws, before fleshing the hide. Hank was surprised at the tender meat, which tasted a lot like beef.

I should note that in addition to the easily disassembled bolt, the Winchester Model 70 has the most dependable type of safety. I've seen the cam-type safety often fail on Remington and Husquevarna rifles, but I know of no safety failures with Winchester, Ruger or Mauser rifles.

The bolts of the Mauser Model 98 and the Ruger Model 77 can be disassembled similar to that of the Winchester Model 70, but not quite so quickly and easily.

Anytime my rifle gets soaked, I disassemble, dry and lubricate the bolt. I also remove the barreled action from the stock for careful cleaning and lubing. Witness marks on the retaining screws allow reassembling the rifle without a change in sighting - important considerations in choosing one's rifle to be used as a tool rather than a showpiece.

Never Cry Raa...

It's rare for a guest hunter to make the ninety minute flight from Kotzebue to the lodge at Trail Creek without seeing at least one Grizzly bear. The big predators have greatly increased in numbers since I first made the trip in 1967. These inland bears tend to be much more aggressive than the coastal brownies whose quest for food is simplified by an abundance of salmon. I advise guests of our bears' ornery nature and always emphasize that they are dangerous game.

Practical jokes are fun, even more if the victim is frightened - in some cases. But joking about bears in bear country is definitely not an acceptable form of humor in my camp.

In the early seventies, I had a small twelve foot by twelve foot plywood cabin which beat any tent in foul weather and offered a modicum of protection from bears. Like any structure in the wilderness, it attracted bears so we were accustomed to seeing fresh tracks and piles of poop nearby. The corners seemed to be growing hair, left by bears that found them to be a convenient rubbing place. Any trip to the outhouse required those answering the call of nature to carry a firearm. I briefed each guest hunter on the wisdom of being armed and alert on their toilet trips, especially if made in the dark. I don't want guests to be overly spooked, but I want them all to be extremely cautious and aware of the possibility of a close encounter with a grizzly.

Two brothers from the midwest named Tom and Tim, had booked for a September hunt. These were a couple of good old farm boys, cajoling and guffawing one another since childhood. Neither missed an opportunity to give the other a hard time. In deplaning the jet in Kotzebue, Tim had turned his ankle and Tom was having a grand time needling his younger brother about the little mishap. Tim tried his best not to show it, but his limp was obviously painful and uncontrollable.

So, for the first day in camp we three took a short hike up the hills on the East side of the valley to glass for game. Tim was in pain, but did not complain. That evening he suggested that he might hang around camp the next day if I thought it a good idea to hunt further down the valley with his brother. Tom told Tim that to limp was manly, but to wimp out on the next day's jaunt was not. Tim grimaced. At times their mutual harassment was a bit too harsh to my way of thinking.

I thought a day of ease would do Tim's ankle a world of good, so Tom and I departed shortly after breakfast for the South Overlook, about three and a half miles down the river.

We got to the vantage point and began scanning the country with our binoculars. Seeing nothing of interest, we ate our sandwiches before Tom dozed off in the warmth of the afternoon sun. A few caribou cows and calves were moving in the valley, but I saw no mature bulls. Dall sheep dotted the higher slopes, but these hunters were after bears and trophy caribou. When Tom woke up we walked a bit further and sat down again to glass. As the sun began to slip behind the highest peaks I saw a grizzly moving along the west bank of Trail Creek. It looked like a decent bear so we bailed off the Overlook and began our stalk.

As is common with bears in the Arctic, this one was foraging along, often disappearing for a few minutes before coming back into sight. It was heading back up stream so our pursuit would get us closer to the cabin as daylight began to wane. About a mile and a half from the runway the bear entered a patch of dwarf birch and slowed down as it slurped up the plentiful soap berries. This delectable (to bears) entree might hold the bear long enough for us to get within range for a shot.

Tom and I carefully threaded our way through the brush and were within less than one hundred yards of the bear when I told him to chamber a round. The bear was a seven footer or so. I chambered one also. I cautioned Tom to hold his fire until the beast continued a bit further as I figured a slight rise in the terrane would expose more of the body for a better shooting opportunity. As the bear began to gain the higher ground, I heard Tom slip off his safety. He brought his rifle to shoulder and was steadily holding when the bear completely disappeared from view. Tom glanced at me and I motioned for him to remain ready and keep watching. We stood in place for a full twenty minutes without catching so much as another glimpse of the critter.

Twilight was compromising our vision, so as I dechambered my cartridge, I whispered to Tom to do the same and that we should retrace our path for a ways, then get on a gravel bar to proceed to the cabin. We might get a chance at the bear on the way back. I was concentrating my gaze on where we had last seen the animal and did not specifically check Tom to see that he had removed the round from his barrel.

And his safety was off.

It took us another hour to go the last mile to the cabin as we slowly walked north anticipating an opportunity at that bear, but we never saw it again.

The adrenalin high we experienced at the possibility of shooting the grizzly had left us tired and somewhat weakened as we walked up the runway toward the willows that surround the cabin. Frost was forming on the tops of the gravel causing the little rocks to stick to the bottoms of our wet boots.

We were clicking along in the fading light. It had been a long day and a tense afternoon. We were tired.

Just as we came around a curve in the trail not fifty yards from the cabin, Tim jumped out in front of us and roared like a growling grizzly. Tom by reflex brought his rifle up leveled at his brother's chest as I yelled "No!"

"Damn you, Tim" Tom hollered.

"Pay back time, brother", retorted Tim, laughing.

I asked Tom to check his rifle, particularly the safety.

"God, Jake, it's got a round in the chamber and it's not on safety" stated Tom.

I sat down along the trail - right there - and told the brothers how lucky we all were that Tom had not shot his brother.

Since that incident I have cautioned all of our guests against doing any "bear scare" antics. Since that day I have double checked to ascertain that barrels are empty after every shooting or near shooting experience. Sometimes I check and verify more than once. It's worth the extra caution.

Emerson's Caribou

Especially when bookings are slow, as sometimes happens, I like to even things up with people that I owe by taking them fishing or hunting.

A friend in Kodiak, Tom Emerson, did quite a lot of work on my aluminum boat, the *F/V LADY SASQUATCH*. I paid the bills as he gave them to me, but they had been too low, in my estimation.

I've always tried to avoid taking too much advantage of anyone, especially good friends, so I told Tom that I was going to go to the bank, get some cash to put in his pocket, or I would buy him a ticket to Kotzebue and then take him hunting for ten days, along with whom ever else was at the lodge during that booking period.

Tom was born and raised in Alaska, but had never been to the far North and was anxious to do it.

When he arrived in Kotzebue, I was there to meet the Alaska Airlines jet. I still had one guest hunting at the lodge who had taken his Grizzly, but Caribou had been few and far between. In fact we had not seen a bull for about a week.

Tom's primary interest was in hunting Willow Ptarmigan, though, and there were plenty around that year. A friend of his had passed away and Tom wound up with his buddy's double barreled, over and under shotgun. He wanted to break it in on birds in the Arctic.

Weather had been deteriorating for the past two days. We were getting mixed rain and snow that September morning, but I thought it was flyable, so we loaded up and headed due north. The flight could be described as a "touchy-feely" one but we did not need to make any unscheduled landings. It took over two hours to get to Trail Creek, rather than the usual ninety minutes. The ground was covered by fresh snow, but at Popple Creek, five miles down stream from the lodge, I began to see fresh trails made by large bands of southerly migrating Caribou. That is always something to stir one's enthusiasm. In situations like that, I feel at least as much excitement as my guests.

Visibility was reduced to about one mile as we landed, and the snow kept falling.

When we walked up to the lodge, the other hunter, Dick, was not to be found. I had no worries about Dick, a very competent outdoors man, in any situation. Soon, he came in off of the eastern foothills and said that he had dropped two bull Caribou.

Conditions began to improve as we three went up to retrieve Dick's animals, but enough snow had fallen to completely cover them. It took us about an hour to locate the two carcasses, then only another hour to cut them in half and pack them back at the meat pole for skinning and bagging. And the Caribou kept coming.

We saw some very good bulls, but Dick said he had enough and Tom could not shoot the same day airborne, so we just watched and drooled.

At times like this, I sometimes wished that guides could hunt for themselves while in company of booked hunters, but the regulation is a good one, and I, of course, had flown that day, too.

Nothing prevents one from making photographs or video the same day airborne, so I set about putting some footage on tape.

Caribou continued to pass by the lodge - all on the east side and moving rapidly along motivated by this initial onset of winter.

I had Tom sight in my spare .300 Winchester Magnum. It was right on the money, as usual.

Tom brought us some fresh ptarmigan that evening, which he and I skinned, then marinated in teriyaki sauce. Fried after being dipped in batter and flour, they were delicious. That is truly a slam dunk for any cook. During his stay he brought us several meals of willow ptarmigan, - or Arctic Chicken.

Caribou were still coming through in groups of dozens to hundreds. Early the next morning I saw a band of seventeen bulls coming toward us, following the same trail that most of the Caribou had used for the past two days. Near the back was a real toad of a bull. I told Tom that was the one

Tom with a batch of Willow Ptarmigan.

we needed to get after. We would have to hustle and forgot to put on the white parkas which had been left drying out in the sauna room.

We rushed out of the lodge and through the willows, crossed the swamp and spotted the band of bulls, still coming our way. The glacier-made moguls in that area are perfect for stalking animals as those natural gullies give the hunters perfect cover. Previous hunters had asked me if we had dug the trenches by hand - they are that handy and uniform.

Tom suggested that since I had never taken a really good bull for myself, that I should shoot that big one. But I declined, explaining the regulations and assuring him that an opportunity would come my way, some day. What a kind offer from him, but it did not surprise me! He's that kind of guy.

When the string of Caribou was as close to us as they would ever get, and offering a broadside shot, Tom dropped the big bull. It's rack was about as good as they come and the old bull was in prime condition with two and a half inches of hard white tallow on the back.

All too soon Dick's time was up. We were going to miss his company and conversation, but the weather was good enough for a trip to town, so I took him along with his trophies and meat to Kotzebue.

Tom and his dandy Caribou.

When I returned, Tom had taken some more ptarmigan - enough for us to each take a couple of packages home after another big meal of the wild chicken.

Before the end of the trip he had taken two more good bulls. All were in prime condition, offering as good a quality meat as exists any where in the world. Taking three Caribou in three shots with my loaner rifle, Tom's marksmanship was deadly.

Those days were as wonderful and carefree as I can recall. Tom said the same. The creeks were full of spawning Char which we photographed and watched, but did not bother as they went about their procreative business.

Before we closed the camp, I spent some time with the tape and scored Tom's first bull. It totaled over 400 SCI points and would likely place in the annual competition, but that was insignificant compared to the overall experience.

The value of some forms of payment far exceeds that of mere money.

Infected Caribou

Wild animals get infections and diseases just as humans and domestic stock do. I've seen very few instances of such problems, probably because they are either soon healed or the animal dies.

When and if a hunter harvests an animal that is obviously diseased, careful thought needs to be given regarding just how to handle the situation. It becomes more complicated if the animal has an admirable trophy quality. Most times, the trophy is taken without any inkling of the hunter that it might be diseased.

Such was the situation that I found myself in one September morning in 1997. My sister, Pat - a Registered Alaskan Guide, and I had some hunting guests at the lodge. Things had been pretty slow. We were seeing plenty of dandy Grizzly bears, but none of the guests had booked for a bear and consequently did not have a permit. Sheep were plentiful, but the area was closed at that time to all but subsistence sheep hunting due to political falderal and the dual management of Alaskan big game by both the Feds and the State. Moose were also available to nonresidents, but only on a drawn permit basis and our guests had no permit, leaving only Caribou, Wolves and Wolverine available to them.

Fog had plagued us the entire season,- thick, heavy, damp, visibility restricting, ground fog visited us daily.

One morning we spotted two bull Caribou grazing on the near edge of the alluvial fan across from the lodge. Everyone gathered up and pulled their hip boots on for a quick hike to the animals.

The stalk was simple. We had only to cross the river, quietly get through a hundred yards of willow brush, get up the cut bank and shoot. Soon, both of the Caribou were down.

When I approached the first and larger bull, I smelled a very disagreeable odor. Cursory inspection revealed a large, goiter-like pus sac at the base of the neck, which was oozing a yellow-greenish pussy exudate. Clearly, such an abscess would be accompanied by a generalized septicemia. The bacteria would have spread throughout the afflicted animal's entire body. In no way were we going to recover the meat from this stinky, sick animal.

However, the rack was very good and the hunter wanted to salvage it and the cape for a shoulder mount.

I slipped on my surgical gloves and caped the beast, telling everyone else to not touch it until I had it completely fleshed and salted. I decided to leave the carcass, minus the head and cape right were it fell, with the abdomen left unopened.

For proof of what we had found and why we did what we did, I took some photos of the carcass which clearly showed the abscess just in front of the left shoulder.

We could at least watch the carcass from the lodge to see what predators or scavengers might feed off of it.

I instructed everyone that should a biologist or game warden arrive, who ever met them first should immediately point out the carcass. Possibly someone would come and take samples before it was too far gone.

From the air this carcass would give one the impression that a stereotypical slob hunter had killed the animal for the rack and cape, wasting all the meat. It appeared to be the remains of an inappropriate, and illegal act.

The second bull was normal in appearance, so we caped it, took the rack and all the meat which was delicious.

Two days went by. I had the hunters a few miles down the creek when the Alaska Department of Fish and Game's protection officer flew over us in a super cub. We all waved, wanting to be seen. The cub landed at the lodge strip and my sister walked over to meet the game cop. This fellow was one of the best game wardens that I have had occasion to deal with, but there have been other good ones, too.

Pat asked if he had seen the carcass.

He said that he had not seen it, so she suggested that he walk over and take some samples of the purulent drainage.

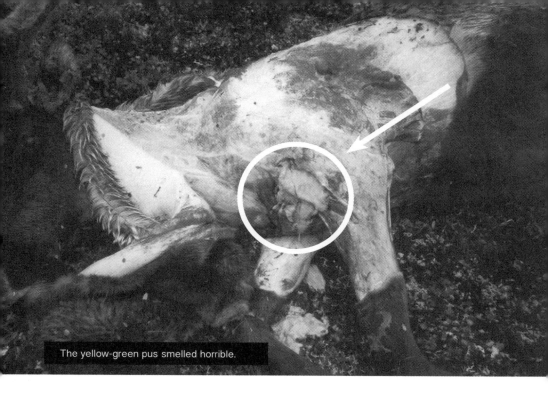

The yellow-green pus smelled horrible.

The game cop did that and came back to tell Pat that he had taken samples and left her his card with a brief description of his findings, adding that we had done the right thing regarding handling of the sick critter. He also said that the hunter could take another Caribou for the meat, but would have to leave the rack of the "make up" animal. (The guest hunters could harvest up to five caribou each, if they had a metal locking tag for each animal in those days).

This was an instance of a righteous government official, doing his job as it was intended to be done.

Privately, I decided that killing one just for the meat was not going to be done. Additional caribou could be taken and fully used, as we normally did.

After another two days, I was again a few miles off with the hunters when the Federal protection aircraft visited Trail Creek. This super cub had a pilot and another official in the back seat. As they turned to land on the strip they noticed the bloated caribou carcass, then pulled up and circled it several times.

As they landed, Pat stopped picking berries on the nearby hillside and walked to meet them. She had her rifle slung over her shoulder, for bear protection.

These guys were in black uniforms with flack jackets and each carried a shotgun in addition to their holstered pistols.

Pat said they looked prepared for trouble and had their shotguns at the ready.

She went through the spiel about the Caribou and suggested that they walk over for a closer inspection. She also showed them the note from the State game cop.

Pat told me that these guys seemed reluctant to have their perceived opportunity for a big arrest dissolving before their eyes. She also told me that they were not at all friendly.

As we always do with protection people, Pat asked for their business cards and insisted that they review all our paperwork, contracts, big game tag sales slips, etc. Everything was in order. These fellows did not bother to walk the half mile to check out the carcass or extract samples. They climbed back into the super cub and departed. Pat said they seemed dejected as they left. Their opportunity for an arrest had evaporated.

We kept an eye on that carcass for weeks and never did we see a bird or other scavenger touch it. It must have been the awful smell that kept even the ravens from feeding on it.

When I got back to Kotzebue I visited both agencies and asked if they communicated with each other. Apparently they didn't have much exchange of information, which is so often the case with government agencies.

So that's how my sister Pat and I handled an obviously contaminated game animal that also had trophy appeal.

Commercial Caribou Hunting in NW Alaska

I first saw Kotzebue, Alaska and the wonderful, nearly virgin wilderness that surrounds it in 1967. I was immediately taken with what seemed to be an unequaled potential for a great, independent, free life, living off the land. A freebooters paradise, it seemed!

Alaskans in Anchorage had told me how non-nutritous Caribou meat was. "A man could starve to death eating Caribou", "Caribou meat is gamey, nothing like good Moose or Sheep", so the commentaries ran. In my extensive travels throughout the region, initially during winter and spring, I was fed Caribou more often than any other meat …. and I quickly developed a preference for it. Normally it was well cooked, most often in stew, but sometimes it was offered frozen and raw by my Eskimo hosts. I liked it any way it was offered. Roasted with fresh seal oil dip was one of the best preparations.

The official Alaska Department of Fish and Game census in 1972 revealed 242,000 animals in the Western Arctic Caribou Herd. Department officials were concerned that this huge number was greater than ever known in past times and over grazing was thought to be a potentially serious threat.

Local folklore and archaeological evidence indicate that in the past, Caribou abundance was followed by extended periods of extreme scarcity, as indicated by a lack of caribou bones, antlers, etc. in middens. This was no doubt motivating biologists to do whatever could be done to avoid a population crash, as Caribou was one of the primary sources of protein for locals of the region.

Continued unlimited harvest, even commercial harvest of Caribou, was believed to serve as an aid in keeping the population in check and keeping a crash from occurring. Caribou season was open all year long with no bag limit.

Exclosures (small plots fenced to eliminate Caribou access) were constructed and monitored on the North Slope and in the Selawik River drainage to enable biologists to evaluate just how serious the overgrazing threat might be. On numerous occasions I flew different biologists out to periodically check the plots, but none seemed alarmed at what we found. Personally, I never noticed a discernible difference between the flora of the exclosures and that of open areas. But it likely would take the skilled evaluation of a specialized botanist to pick up on any but the most obvious evidence of overgrazing.

Annual Caribou census efforts in Northwest Alaska were intensified, beginning in 1975 due to an apparent, abrupt decrease in the numbers of Rangifer tarandus.

So, prior to 1976, Caribou hunting in that area remained unrestricted, with no closed season and no bag limit. Commercial harvesting of wild Caribou was allowed and a clean, head or neck shot carcass was worth about thirty-five dollars in Kotzebue, depending on it's condition. Several commercial hunters in the area made some serious money, albeit for short periods of time, primarily in the spring, as huge herds of Caribou migrated from wintering grounds in the south to the primary calving location on the North Slope, located just a bit north of our lodge.

For a couple of years, my wife, Mae, and I engaged in some commercial spring hunts, our goal being to take ten or more Caribou each day, as I could fit that many properly prepared cow carcasses in our Cessna 180 which was fitted with hydraulic wheel skis. If we took more than we could haul in a single load, the extras were gutted, beheaded, with legs bound into a nice package using rubber bands made from truck tire inner tubes or short pieces of rope, and left belly down to discourage birds from pecking at the fresh meat. Left that way, ravens and sea gulls would feed on the exposed gut pile rather than try to get at the good meat. Once frozen in proper form, a carcass could be stacked nicely in the airplane. I removed the front passenger seat and the rear seats and left them at home. Three carcasses could be placed in the front and the rest just aft of the pilot seat, giving the aircraft a favorable weight and balance.

On more than one occasion we commented to each other that this was "buffalo hunting" as we never expected to see in our lifetime.

The technique was to find a band of Caribou crossing a sufficiently large stretch of smooth snow or a large lake which was good for landing on skis. I would land the airplane so as to split the herd, then we would jump out and start shooting animals. Usually one component of the herd would run off, while the other trailing group would mill about, offering easy targets. Under ideal circumstances we could stack up a plane load or more on a single landing. Head shots were preferred and insured the top price for the carcass. On one such landing we downed 47 Caribou, requiring five trips to town with the Cessna loaded to maximum capacity each trip. In the early 1970s, with aviation gasoline available at about fifty cents a gallon, a load of ten Caribou made good economic sense, if the flying time was not too long.

We got a lot of practice in all aspects of the harvest. We could remove the head and lower legs and have the guts out in less than ten minutes per animal. We saved the heart, but not the liver (Cesium - a fallout contaminant from Russian nuclear air bursts was concentrated in the livers and I deemed it best to avoid) or other parts of the entrails. We kept our knives sharp and used a small file to freshen up the edge while in the field. We seldom knicked our fingers and never had a serious self-inflicted accidental wound in these operations.

On occasion, returning to a kill site, we would find wolves or wolverine enjoying the feast, so they, too, were open game and were added to the year's collection of furs.

I occasionally was tortured by thoughts about the ethics of taking animals this way, but after expressing my misgivings to a friendly game warden, he loaned me a book about Deer Stalking in New Zealand. Hunters there were paid a bounty for tails of Red Deer. Little concern was given to the meat, unless the kill was located in a spot handy for meat utilization. Most of the deer were just shot and left. Wanton waste laws prevented that in Alaska, thank goodness.

I reasoned that if such practices were encouraged in a modern country like New Zealand, our technologically enhanced harvesting, using aircraft and recovering the meat for human consumption was certainly a far better way to handle overpopulation of any species. So, I laid my doubts to rest and got with the program.

Mae and I enjoyed this activity until 1974, when I noticed what I believed to be a significant decrease in caribou numbers. I ceased harvesting more caribou than we and our close friends and relatives could personally consume. We no longer took caribou to sell.

In NW Alaska in the spring of 1976, large numbers of caribou were found dead in the tundra. Hundreds had been shot and left without being used. A research team from the University of Alaska and biologists from the Alaska Department of Fish and Game verified that most of the wasted Caribou had been shot with .223 solid (military) bullets. The Alaska National Guard had armories in most of the villages and it was apparent that Guard rifles and ammunition had been used.

This was appalling to all who witnessed or learned of it.

A biologist presented the findings to the Department, but he was essentially "muzzled" as such unconscionable waste was shocking to everyone and the administration wanted to avoid a scandal. The massive waste was nevertheless documented and other sites with similar slaughters were discovered. Several thousand Caribou had been shot and left in the field during April, 1976 in northwestern Alaska.

In late May and early June of 1976, an intensive census was conducted with multiple aircraft and several biologists involved, myself included.

It had been suggested that the huge drop in caribou numbers might be due to retention of the placenta at the time of birthing. This abnormality would quickly lead to the death of the cow and, subsequently, the calf.

Flying for the Alaska Department of Fish and Game, I spent weeks with a biologist in the back seat of my super cub, cruising with full flaps at low speed just above the rumps of caribou. We were looking for signs of retained placentas in the cows, but we never found a one.

The result of the census indicated that the Caribou herd had plummeted from nearly a quarter of a million animals to about 75,000 or possibly less!

Rural Alaska had a crisis! Recriminations were cast primarily against commercial hunters and non-local, white, sport hunters. The Caribou limit was reduced to one per year, per person and cows were protected from spring until fall. The news of the overkill and gross wastage of carcasses was never made public.

Ready to land, commercial Caribou hunting.

Caribou are the most successfully adapted to the Arctic of all big game animals. Continued monitoring and census work revealed a recruitment of about thirteen percent per year.

No new sites of massive slaughter were reported and by the mid-1980s, the WAH caribou numbers had rebounded to surpass that of 1972 (242,000). The Caribou bag limit was raised to fifteen animals per person -PER DAY - for local residents and five animals per person PER DAY for other Alaskan residents, with a limit of five animals per year for nonresident and alien hunters. However commercial caribou hunting was no longer allowed, nor was the sale of caribou meat or parts - officially, that is.

New subsistence regulations made it handy for local people to trade their surplus Caribou meat and eventually, federal money was available for local hunters to purchase fuel and ammunition for harvesting Caribou for elders and others unable to hunt for themselves.

An Early 1970s Sheep Hunt

One of the first guided sheep hunts I did as a newly licensed Registered Guide was with a retired steel worker, Nick, from Pittsburgh. He was a blue collar, gnarly knuckled fellow, accustomed to hard labor and crowded urbanity. In his first telephone conversation, he made it clear that he wanted a true wilderness experience in the Brooks Range of Alaska's Arctic. He told me that he was less concerned with the size of his ram, than with a bare knuckle bout with nature. He wanted to live off the land on his hunt and if in the end he did not even get a shot at a ram, he could be happy with the trip, so long as it was done "like in the old days." If he was to take a ram, he wanted to earn it by his strictly personal definition of "honestly".

Intrigued, I mentioned that unnecessary hardship was to be avoided, as in the normal course of events we generally encounter enough of that, anyway. I told him of a place, inaccessible to most, that I thought would satisfy his dreams. We would fly out to my cabin, then strike off afoot with my black lab, Zeke. The dog would be good bear security at night as well as a great companion at all times. I could make a couple of air drops containing candy, hot chocolate, flour, jerky, dried fish, coffee and other staples. We would "siwash it" with minimal comforts.

Nick told me that I needn't drop any food as far as he was concerned. I made two drops, anyway.

Old Murphy must have felt kindly towards us, as when Nick's time came, the weather was wonderful. He arrived in Kotzebue on a late flight, so we put him up on the couch at home. The next morning was warm with great visibility, so we flew up to the cabin in the super cub, with Nick contentedly holding Zeke on his lap.

Earlier that summer I had seem a big ram with one horn heavily broomed hanging out alone two drainages west, near Mount Bastille, which was too far for most hunters to travel, but should satisfy this guest. As we flew through the mountains to the cabin, Nick got a chance to see what he was in for and he was enthusiastic. Following some shots to check his rifle, Nick was excited to get started.

After tying down the plane and stowing some gear in the cabin we started early that afternoon. At the end of the runway I glassed a big ram in West Bowl, so put the spotting scope on it. It was a dandy, bigger than average and over a full curl, but Nick said that one would be too easy, so we continued packing on down Trail Creek, cut across the big pucker brush flat and camped for the night on Popple Creek, about five miles from the cabin. We carried some jerky, salmon strips, candy bars, apples, sandwiches, and bug dope. We were going to rough it, but I wanted to avoid some of the extremes, so I included a roll of toilet paper - I knew that I, at least, would chose it over naturally available rocks or leaves.

The lemming population was high that year, with lots of well defined trails all through our route. Zeke was pretty adept at catching them, always bringing them to me alive, often squeaking. I would take the little critters from the dog, praise him and release them. Zeke seemed to question my action, but never lost his enthusiasm for "mousing". I had packed Zeke's saddle bags with dog food, but that did not seem to impair his pursuit and capturing of the little rodents.

The next evening we were at the base of Mount Bastille. Glassing revealed no sheep, but several large caribou bulls were meandering in the high meadows. A big Grizzly sow and her three cubs were working the hillside about a mile from our camp site, oblivious to our incursion into their territory.

I spotted the surveyor's tape flagging one of the air drops, but did not mention it to Nick.

Another peaceful night was followed by a clear, chilly morning. We climbed to a point that offered good glassing, but could not find a sheep. I knew that rams frequented the area that time of year, so we started up into the higher country, going slow, expecting to locate sheep. Three caribou bulls in a hanging meadow rose and watched us as we ascended toward

Zeke and, later, Max were the best dogs I've ever had.

the rocky crags near the summit. Still no sheep. Nick was not discouraged, rather, he seemed to become more enthusiastic with every step.

We topped out and sat glassing until I found three rams high on a slope across the next drainage. This was going to be a real pull over and back, hopefully returning with a sheep, but Nick, in his mid sixties, was holding up fine, so we headed down to make camp near the stream below the ridge that held the rams. It had become noticeably cooler, so I scraped out two pits about six feet in length and eighteen inches wide in the sand near the stream, placed dead willow branches in each and lit fires. We cooked stick bread on the fires and heated some water for chocolate. Our sandwiches were gone and we were running low on jerky and dried fish.

Zeke brought me another lemming which Nick thought looked enticing, so, what the heck, I figured. I prepared it and skewered it on a stick to roast. With a little salt and pepper it was tasty, in fact it was delicious. So, thanks to Zeke, we had three more, - each. The dog's wagging tail indicated his approved of this use of his catches.

One has to be careful to not over cook those little rodents. We supplemented our meat dish with some roots called "masu, or Eskimo potatoes" that are common that time of year in the sandy reparian areas. Some blue berries, along with crow berries and cranberries made a fine, if somewhat spartan dessert.

Once the bed fires had burnt down to coals, I covered the depressions with sand and we laid our space blankets on top, with a second blanket covering each of us. We slept pleasantly. Zeke curled up, as usual, near my midsection, added to my warmth and comfort.

Northern lights entertained us that night and Nick said that this was indeed, what he had come to Alaska to experience.

Early the next morning, we sighted the rams bedded near the skyline. After close scrutiny with the spotting scope, it was apparent that none of the rams was exceptional, but two were legal. I figured the big one I'd seen previously to be one of the commonly encountered sub species, - Ovis disappearacus. We loaded our gear and made our way toward the now feeding sheep. By mid afternoon I was convinced that these were the only sheep on the mountain and suggested that we head back toward Trail Creek in hopes of finding the broomer near the cabin. Nick said that no ram of any size could please him more than one of those that we had gone so far to get. He added that he was ready to taste fresh sheep meat.

An overcast sky and southerly wind suggested that we might soon have adverse weather to deal with, so I agreed that he should take the best of the rams which was a shade less than full curl, - legal in those days. Our stalk took us to within 80 yards of the rams, with Zeke crawling on his belly, as we did. Nick shot true and the ram obliged us by rolling down hill on the route we would prefer to take on our way back. Nick insisted on carrying half of the meat, along with the head and cape of his ram. I expected no less of him.

Before dark we were back at our last fire/sleeping pits, - this time roasting sheep ribs instead of lemmings. I had placed a section of small intestine, squeezed free of it's contents, and some other special goodies, in my bag. That evening I rinsed out the intestine in the clear cold creek, tied a knot in one end and placed chopped heart, liver, fat and bits of meat mixed with some powdered chili, salt and pepper inside, tied the other end and roasted "campfire" sausages. It was wild man's meat for sure, and tasted wonderful.

The hard earned meat in combination with our hunger, would make anyone seem like a great chef.

When you're hungry and burning a lot of energy, fat tastes good, especially when roasted to a crispy state over a fire. Those sheep ribs were as good as they get - maybe because we were so hungry and tired, but I think they would have been just as welcome in any situation. We consumed all the ribs, with Zeke's willing help.

A few rain showers visited us that dark overcast night, but it had warmed up and we slept well. Morning found us drinking the last of the coffee. In fact we had consumed all of our grub, except for the sheep meat, so tenderloins and a piece of backstrap with fat left on, made our breakfast.

Two men sharing the load of one ram is not a bad pack and we made good time up over the divide and down to our second night's camp. Nick liked the idea of sleeping warmer than he had on the previous night, so he set about preparing the two trenches while I went to retrieve the air drop package, containing flour, coffee, hot chocolate and candy bars, which Nick was pleased to see …. and share. I'd wrapped the drop package in newspapers and small pieces of foam, that served us as spartan bedding supplements. We enjoyed hot chocolate, stick bread, and candy bars along with more roasted sheep backstrap. The night was clear and once again we were entertained by the aurora borealis. Zeke's growling woke me about 3:00 am, but I decided he was irritated by the aurora, rather than a bear, - or it might have been Nick's snoring.

We followed Popple Creek to a stand of cottonwood trees near where I had dropped the other package, but long before we reached the spot, I could see that something - a bear or wolverine most likely - had beaten us to it. It looked like the package had exploded. Nothing was usable. I gathered up the mess and burned it on a gravel bar. We decided to go on back to the cabin as the full moon made travel easy and the thought of a can of beans followed by a bed with a full foam mattress was appealing to both of us.

Though our loads were becoming lighter with every meal, our packs seemed heavier as we made the last few miles. The sight of the cabin at

4:00 am was most welcome. I made a fire in the Franklin stove and Nick produced a small jug of whiskey to top off the day.

Nick had the experience he had dreamed of and I had enjoyed one of the finest hunting pursuits of my life, shared with two of my favorite companions.

Published in the *Alaska Professional Hunter*, Spring/Summer Issue, 2011

Single Horner in Skolai Pass

I n the late 1960s and early 1970s I worked as Assistant Guide for my good friend, Jim Cann. He had a tent camp for sheep hunting in Skolai Pass which is in the Wrangell Mountains. The short, bumpy strip was at just over 5,000 feet elevation and he managed big loads in and out of there with bush pilot skill such as I had not seen prior to working for him. At that altitude, I learned that leaning the mixture would produce extra RPMs from the 150 hp Lycoming engine, which no doubt could make the difference between a successful take off and a serious pile up. He kept his cub in top mechanical shape, which coupled with his superior abilities allowed him to access this marginal spot and others, some of which were much closer to the edge of the envelope of a super cub's performance.

The area around Skolai Pass consistently produced superior quality rams, with forty inchers always a possibility.

Before I had an airplane, I would drive Jim's 1955 Chevy pickup loaded with supplies to Chitina. Later, I used my Cessna 180 to get myself and supplies to Chitina. He would fly the camp in, then me, to set up the cooking tent and two sleeping tents while he ferried sheep hunters in one at a time. Normally we had two sheep hunters per booking period but occasionally there would be three guest hunters. Caribou and black bears were infrequent transients in the Pass. Resident willow ptarmigan were plentiful. Until snow began to lock up the country, it was a great place to seek a really big ram, and to spend time.

In August, 1969 we had three hunters at the Pass. One especially fit young cabinet maker was set on taking a forty inch ram or nothing at all. This fellow was not at all egotistical about it. But he was determined.

We spent the first two days in a group, glassing sheep within a day's walk of the camp. The best rams we found were in a group of three. The longest horn we saw was well past a curl and about 38 inches in length, a beautiful head, but for the fact that one side was broken off just below the tip of the boss. We called it the "single horner". An unusually wide full curl and an average full curl ram stayed close to the single horner.

Jim decided to take the cabinet maker on a three to five day jaunt to the northeast, across some glaciers to an isolated area that had produced some big rams in the past. The other two hunters and I made day trips out of the main camp, looking over new areas each day.

After a week, we had found nothing to beat the two rams that accompanied the single horner, so the decision was made to go after them before Jim and his hunter returned.

My hunters were an older cowboy named Dick and his son in law, Jerry. Dick pronounced it Geery. Dick said he would be happy to tag the ram with the wide horns, which he called the "longhorn". The son in law said he'd settle for the other, more typical full curl ram.

A little snow had fallen and some low clouds occluded the higher terrane, but we headed for the band of sheep, expecting breaks in the cloud cover to allow us to locate and approach the animals.

We found the rams, but clouds kept moving through, sometimes covering the area that held the sheep. We were headed up the slope that our quarry occupied when dense fog moved in and enveloped the mountain. I figured we could get above the place we last saw the sheep and be in position to shoot, if and when it cleared. The breeze strengthened and as it cleared off the fog, the rams had moved uphill and were above us at less than 100 yards. I looked them over and told Dick to shoot the longhorn on the far left and Jerry to take the ram on the far right. Dick's ram went down. The other two startled, and not having seen or smelled us, began to mill around. I told Jerry that his ram was again on the right side, but he shot the left one - the single horn ram. That ram staggered and began to limp away. Jerry was then aiming at the third ram. I told him to finish the crippled sheep, so he shot it again. Then realizing his mistake he let out a howl. Rats, we had mentioned and joked about how some poor devil would probably kill the single horner and have only half a trophy. Murphy's luck was with us that day, as usual!

Dick was excited, but Jerry was feeling bad. After checking out his ram, Dick went over to Jerry, slapped him on the back and said "Don't worry

Dick and his "long horn", Skolai Pass 1969

Dick and his "long horn", me with the one horner.

Geery, ye kin always mount it on the wall, like a feesh!" That comment broke the spell for Jerry and we all had a good laugh. That evening I commented that the ribs of the single horner tasted just as good as those of the longhorn.

In a couple of days Jim and the cabinet maker returned with no sheep. They had seen two rams of potentially forty-one or forty-two inch horn length, but had not been able to get close enough for a shot.

I guess half a sheep is better than no sheep, especially on the dinner table.

The Heart of a Ram

In 1982 I had begun a major addition to my home in Kotzebue. I'd been working on the plans throughout the previous winter. My materials were ordered from Seattle and arrived on the first barge in mid July. Shortly after receiving the shipment, my friend Bruce Moe, his son Jason and a two framers came up to see to getting the project enclosed with the steel roof in place, so that I could finish it off during the coming winter.

Those Seattle guys were accustomed to working hard and efficiently and we had a 36 foot by 44 foot second story room framed on over the top of part my existing ground floor. A pony wall allowed the original roof to remain in place, causing minimal disruption of our home activities. Outside buttresses supported an overhang on both sides of the new room. It was the biggest and most complex addition that I had done, but to those guys it was pretty routine. Weather cooperated and in three days it was enclosed, windows set and the steel roof was on.

I was active throughout those super productive days keeping the materials flowing and supplies handy to allow the professionals to do their thing without unnecessary distractions. I'd never before seen such carpenterial efficiency! I had ten days yet before our first guest hunters were to arrive, so I was putting in sixteen hour days to expedite the project in hope and expectation of completing it by Thanksgiving.

Dall sheep season opened on August 10. When my two guests arrived on August 8, I was relieved to be going sheep hunting, - just so I could rest.

Bob and Ray were Florida fern growers and very pleasant southern gentlemen who came with hopes of each bagging a Dall Ram, Moose and Caribou.

Weather remained nice and since I had more sheep hunters coming that season, I decided to take these fellows to an area half the distance to the lodge, thereby saving the sheep closer to the lodge for later and worse weather. We would use a single four man tent and hopefully have their rams within the first two or three days.

My most reasonable access to the hunting area required landing the cub on a cut bank covered in knee high "pucker brush", bordered on each side by a four foot drop off. The middle of the strip narrowed down to just wide enough for the main tires of the cub. An error of three feet to the right or left would result in a bad wreck. We called that strip "the coke bottle".

With Ray in the back seat, along with the tent, food and some gear, I looked that hazardous airfield over several times before committing. We got landed with a few bounces and some fresh green brush marks on the tail and propeller, but it was good enough. I trimmed some brush before sticking small pieces of toilet paper on some of the dwarf birch bushes to mark the narrows and the threshold. Then I went back for Bob.

With the plane tied down, tent up and camp secure, we walked down the creek and caught some fresh Arctic Char for dinner that night. We could see sheep on both sides of the creek and expected shooting opportunities the next morning. It was a beautiful evening there, 120 miles above the Arctic Circle.

By 8:00 am of opening day we were on a high ridge east of the tent deciding which route to take to put us onto a band of five nice rams when two super cubs that I did not recognize, one blue and the other red, came flying through the area, just above the top of the peaks. One of the pilots banked hard left and buzzed the rams we were watching, sending the sheep up and over the skyline - away from us.

My yellow cub and the tent must have been easily visible to the cub drivers, but they continued to work up and down each side canyon, then they flew to the west side and did the same. I was boiled! It appeared that they were intentionally hazing the sheep and interfering with our hunt.

After more than 30 minutes of this activity, the strange cubs flew off to the north.

Bob, Ray and I hunted the rest of the day, but found no rams on the mountain. I did pick up some interesting fossils at 3,800 feet. The ancient cone snails and shells had formed eons ago on the bottom of a warm coral sea, but now were lying about in sheep country.

August 11 was spent in quest of rams on the west side of the valley, but we found nothing large enough to pursue, so I took Bob to the lodge where my Dad, sister Pat, and labrador, Max, were waiting. I introduced Bob, then went back, struck the camp and picked up Ray.

Pop and Pat said they had seen the Blue and Red cubs two days before as they flew overhead, going north. We did not see either of those planes again, I am happy to say.

Moose and Caribou were in good numbers around the lodge and each guest collected those species. We all enjoyed the fresh game meat.

We glassed three full curl rams feeding on Middle Mountain, easily visible from the lodge windows, so we decided to have a go at them.

I wondered if Bob had been a cowboy as his legs were noticeably bowed, but he told me that as a child he had suffered from rickets. Walking was somewhat stressful for him, but, as it is with so many avid hunters, he ignored his discomfort. He had heart.

When we got to the ridge cresting Middle Mountain the rams had moved further east and seemed agitated. They were not running, but were covering ground faster than we could.

Knowing that we could not catch them, we sat down and had our sandwiches. Shortly thereafter the rams stopped to feed on the sparse vegetation up ahead and one of the bigger rams bedded down. This was the signal to ramp up our efforts, which we did, taking care to keep out of sight of the sheep and close the distance between them and us.

It was past supper time with dark coming on when we finally were within range. Ray's ram took a hit in the withers and rolled down the hill.

Bob's ram was hit just a whisker aft of perfect, but it rolled, too. As we walked toward them, Bob's got up and started running. Bob's next three shots were off the mark and the bloodied ram was out of sight.

Leaving Ray with his trophy, Bob and I side hilled after his, which had found new strength and was by then climbing up a shale slide across the canyon from us. Bob hit him again and again it rolled down the slope, only to get up and began to slowly climb back up the hill.

By now after being knocked down twice, this ram was slowed down enough to allow Bob and I to gain ground on him and as the ram reached a rocky outcropping, Bob put another one into him and the sheep came rolling back toward us. This time it did not get up.

We took photos and as I was caping the ram, Bob told me that he wasn't certain he would have a shoulder mount made, but for sure I should bring it's heart for Bob's taxidermist to mount. I shared that sentiment.

Bob, the ram with "Heart" & Jake.

We loaded the sheep onto my pack and went back to Ray, who was about three quarters of a mile back down the drainage. I set at caping, then butchering the second ram and put that meat in my pack, too. Bob and Ray carried their heads and capes. We were all tired, but very contented. A Dall ram was the trophy most important to Bob and Ray.

Ray, his Ram & Jake...plumb dark.

Most of the walking was down country, but there was the last series of hills to climb before reaching Trail Creek and the lodge. With shoulders and feet aching, we took some short naps as we returned.

The sun had long since retired in our area, but with a cloudless sky, we had enough light to pick our way through the boulders, brush and tussocks without too many stumbles.

It was sure good to reach the comforts of the lodge, well after sunup the next morning.

Bob and I will never forget the heart of that ram.

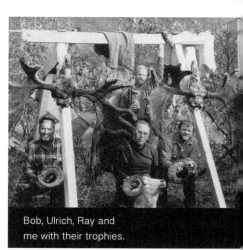

Bob, Ulrich, Ray and me with their trophies.

My Best Ram

Forty inches of horn length is sort of the holy grail for dedicated North American sheep hunters. Most rams do not have the genetic ammunition to produce that much horn, fewer still live long enough and/or have the nutritional abundance to culminate in such growth.

Long before coming to Alaska, I'd been aware of the magic forty inch figure for sheep. After getting into the guiding business, I watched the Alaska Department of Fish and Game annual reports in the 1970s and noted that of the approximately 1,000 rams harvested per year, usually ten or fewer made or exceeded 40 inches in horn length.

While serving as Assistant Guide for Jim Cann in the Wrangle Mountains, "forty inchers" were often mentioned. Our base camp was in Skolai Pass and the area had consistently produced good rams in the forty inch plus class. Some of the guest hunters we had during my time with Jim took such trophies, but my best ram from hunts in the Chugach, Wrangles and Brooks Range had thirty-eight and a half inches of horn length. Not bad, but I longed for a bigger one.

In 1972 I became a Registered Guide and began to book hunters of my own for the Western Brooks Range, north of my home in Kotzebue. I missed the bigger country of the Wrangels, but had come to love my own area even more.

In late August, 1974,when I returned to town after closing up the lodge for ten days, until the next booked hunters were to arrive, I had a message on the answering machine. It was from Jim Cann and he barely whispered into his phone as he told me he'd found some outstanding rams, two of which with big bases, he estimated to be over 45 inches in horn length. But they were too far from camp for his guest hunters to go. He had left the tents in place and was back in Anchorage, but would like to go back as soon as possible, to make an attempt at those huge rams. And, could I come down to make the trip with him? I called him immediately. He said it would be best if I brought the Cessna 180 to Anchorage, then we'd take it and his Super Cub to Chitina, leave my plane there and go to Skolai Pass in his cub. When we were done, he'd ferry me and the camp gear back to Chitina, then we'd fly to Anchorage and I could come home. Considering the urgency of the situation and the relatively late date, I said I'd shower, pack and come down that same night. Weather was favorable with clear sky and a full moon. I could come directly over the top of the Alaska Range and be in Anchorage well before daylight.

I'd felt tired when I got home, but this news rejuvenated me beyond expectation. I did as planned, landed at Merrill Field, crawled into the back of the plane and slept until Jim woke me up about 7:00 am. We had breakfast at Peggy's Cafe, divided the food and other supplies, and departed for Chitina before 9:00 am. We slept that evening in the tent at Skolai Pass. What a distance and change it was from where I'd been less than 24 hours before!

Weather was still good when we started for the big rams early the next morning. There were two major drainages to cross before camping the next night on a glacier. We put in most of a second day to get within walking distance of where Jim had last seen the rams. A quick binocular survey revealed the same band of rams and the spotting scope certified the quality of the two largest ones. We were both excited, but worn out and the distance too far to do yet that same day.

So we set up the tent, had a warm dinner and went to sleep.

But the wind came up and snow began falling just before midnight. By morning we had near zero visibility and eight inches of fresh, wet snow on the tent. I had a paperback book to read and Jim smoked his pipe most of that day, as the snow steadily accumulated. The snowfall was certainly cause for concern, but as our return route would at least take us to lower elevations, we decided to wait it out for another day.

On day four of the trip snow was still coming down, but slower. The sky was a sullen gray and promised more of the white stuff. Reluctantly, we decided it best to start packing out of the area before it became too hazardous. As we trudged back, slipping and stumbling into holes obscured by the snow, I kept looking back, but what I saw only served to convince me that we were correct in aborting the trip. Had we radio communications and a accurate forecast, we would never have begun.

But, as in all such endeavors, the most important thing to get is BACK!

After a strenuous two days, the camp in Skolai Pass was a welcome sight. It took half of the following day to clear and pack the snow on the small strip sufficiently for Jim to take me and some of the gear out. He returned and made a second trip to Chitina, where my Cessna was tied down.

We set up the tent and spent a night in that tiny town.

Our return to Anchorage was relatively uneventful, as was my trip back to Kotzebue.

I continued to dream of taking a forty incher.

In 1976 the Western Arctic Caribou Herd had dwindled from about a quarter of a million animals to somewhere between fifty and seventy-five thousand. I had been contracted in May to fly my Super Cub for the Alaska Department of Fish & Game, primarily for Caribou census work. Most of the census effort was exerted in early June in the areas close to the annual calving grounds, about 40 miles north of our lodge.

Later, in July, having not come up with the expected numbers, we did "search surveys" throughout the region. These special efforts were disappointing as well. On one such special trip, my assigned sector included the high mountains just West of our lodge. Previous flights through that sector had led me to call it the "salad fork" of that river, as there was seldom any meat on it. We had been seeing only a few scattered Caribou, mostly singles or lone cows with a calf. (Twinning is rare in Caribou.) I gained altitude to look around a high cliff area that caribou sometimes frequented and saw some sheep, so I pulled a notch of flaps to slow down and look more closely. WOW! Two monster rams the like of which I had never seen in the Brooks Range were lying near the top. Both appeared to have well over forty inches in horn length. One ram was seriously broomed on one horn, the other was not broomed at all and looked like it carried an honest curl and a quarter.

A second pass verified what I thought I'd seen the first time around. I never flew too close to animals of any species, thinking that I might cause them to depart the area. I certainly did not want to alarm these old rams.

But how was I to get at them? The nearby canyons were narrow, twisted, and steep sided, offering no place to land. Landing on any of those slopes was out of the question. But I knew exactly where those rams were and expected them to remain there, unmolested. I had to figure a way to get myself to them.

It was still a month from the opening of sheep season and I pondered this dilemma daily. I made two more trips to be sure that the rams had not left their crags and to scrutinize the area for a place to land. The big sheep stayed put, but I found no access.

I had a couple of sheep hunters due on August 8, to begin their hunt on August 10, but they called, saying they needed to delay their hunt by a week. As no one was booked for the next week, I suggested they come on Aug. 18 and stay until the end of the month, giving them a better chance to include Moose and/or Caribou in their bag. They liked that proposal. These fellows were fit, but not up to walking from the lodge to the "salad fork" location.

I had advised the Alaska Department of Fish and Game that I had hunters arriving on Aug. 8 and could not do any flying for them after that date, so I was free. I tortured myself with thoughts of those big rams. I knew that this might be the best or only chance I would have at such a magnificent sheep. It was worth a maximum effort. I contacted three friends individually, asking if they were up for a strenuous sheep hunt, mentioning that I had located a couple of dandies, but for various reasons none could make the time for that hunt.

However, I had my very fine Labrador, Zeke, who packed well and could make the trip with me.

I put together some air drops, consisting of candy bars, nuts, jerky, dried fish (salmon, pike & white fish), dried fruit, instant oatmeal, salt, pepper, cayenne powder, coffee, hot chocolate, and of course, dog food. On August 7, I loaded Zeke into the cub, along with the provisions and camp gear and headed to the lodge. I dropped Zeke at the lodge, as he always got nervous when I opened the clam shell door to do the air drops. After

Zeke and later, Max, were willing to carry a load.

making the drops we spent the night at the lodge, in high anticipation of the forthcoming trip.

Zeke and I had made a similar trip a few years before with a guest hunter for a ram and we had been successful. This trip was to require at least another day walking each way, but I felt up to it, and Zeke, of course, was more than willing.

Daylight comes early that time of year in that area, 165 miles north of the Arctic Circle, but neither the dog nor I had slept deeply and we were up and hiking before 5:00 am. So we headed north, through a pass about five miles upstream, then around the northern rim of the range, crossing several streams near their headwaters.

Mosquitoes weren't too pestiferous, but the temperatures were in the high sixties to the mid seventies, with only slight thermal breezes. Both my dog and I got hot early on. I took off my under wear and T-shirt, traveling in a pair of denim jeans and an unbuttoned long sleeved shirt. Before noon we had run into a herd of about 120 Caribou, the largest bunch I had seen since just after the calving time nearly two months before. These animals were clustered on a snow bank on the western slope of a steep canyon and could easily have been missed by anyone doing an aerial survey.

I did not carry a spotting scope this trip, considering the distance and all, but I had a small pair of Zeiss 10X20 binoculars which allowed me to identify several other rams that I had not seen from the air. I scrutinized them, to be sure that I wasn't passing up either of the two monsters, and kept plugging on toward the salad fork.

Camp the first night was on a small creek with me lying on a space blanket without making a fire coal bed, as it was plenty warm. I did put on my T-shirt, down vest and jacket before covering up with a second space blanket. The dog tucked in beside me and we slept for short periods, but comfortably. Zeke was never prone to barking, but he was quick to growl if he detected an alien smell or sound, so I had little concern for bears.

Another early start put us within glassing distance of the big rams' hangout by the next evening. This northern route was a quicker one than the one I'd taken years before. If I connected with a ram, the return to the cabin would be considerably easier than I had expected. Zeke and I spent that night as we had the previous one.

The third morning we walked to the western aspect of the area to glass. The jagged crags that had held those rams were cut with deep crevasses, any one of which could conceal several animals, so I planned to spot the sheep from below, then decide on an approach.

Early in the afternoon I located the two rams, not five hundred yards from where I'd last seen them. They were bedded high on the ridge with a commanding view of the country below. I saw no other sheep in the area, which I figured a was good thing as there would be fewer eyes to see Zeke and me.

Leaving all but my meat board, rifle, water jug, candy bars, and camera, Zeke and I worked our way up a gut just downwind of the bedded rams. It took only two hours of slow climbing, then we settled in to see if an opportunity would present itself.

Sheep can subsist in areas which appear to be devoid of any vegetation, nibbling small patches of mountain dryass or whatever is available, but they periodically descend to greener areas to feed, then retire to more secure bedding areas. After about three hours of dozing on the hillside,

I looked up and saw that the ram with the broomed left horn had risen. He stretched and began to amble downhill. The horn bases were more massive than those of his partner, but he did not have quite the length. He was soon followed by the other ram, and they slowly fed toward my dog and me. Zeke saw them and nudged me with his nose. I patted his head and whispered "quiet" to him. At 300 yards I centered my cross hairs on each ram. I was sure the broomed ram would score higher, but I decided on the other. The broomer fed down into a gut and was out of sight. I felt confident that I could take the other at that range, but if they both disappeared into the gut, I could move in to reduce the distance by half or more, unless they did something unexpected. I waited until the second ram fed out of sight, then rose and carefully made my way to the edge of the gut with Zeke at my left heel.

When I got to the edge of the gut, both rams were feeding below me at about 60 yards, unconcerned, on my side of the gully, with their backs to me! I carefully glassed them both over again, then steadied on the withers of the one I wanted and squeezed. The bullet's impact literally drove the ram into the ground, nose first. He appeared to have been pole axed! The other ram jerked his head up and looked right at us, then made several jumps up the slope and stopped to look at us again. Zeke whined and looked at me. I told him "No, Stay". The broomed ram began to steadily walk away, occasionally looking back at us and at his partner, which had not moved since the shot.

I sat down and stroked my dog as the second ram, never running, just walked up the slope and into one of the rocky chimneys.

Within a few minutes the live ram was out of sight, occasionally showing glimpses of his white rump hair as he climbed into the crags.

Our ram was lying as if he was sleeping on his belly with his nose in the rocks. He was magnificent! I knew I would probably never have such an opportunity again.

The .300 Winchester Magnum hand loaded, 150 grain bullet had struck just where I'd aimed, breaking the spine and plowing through the chest cavity to stop in the brisket. Every foot pound of energy had been absorbed by that old ram and I'm sure he never knew what hit him. It had been lights out, period.

I had brought only a cheap, small camera, as was usual for me those days. I took several pictures of the ram alone and with Zeke, then got at caping the trophy. I boned the meat, leaving the scapula and femur in place and took the rib cages intact. The ram was a bit less in body size than average, but it still made a pretty weighty load. He was fat and in superb condition overall.

We got to the spot where I'd left the rest of our stuff and went on a few hundred yards to a decent place close to a small creek for the night. This time I gathered up a fair pile of dead willows and as soon as it had burned down to coals, I leaned a side of ribs on some green branches over the heat and let it bake. A little salt and pepper made a magnificent supper for Zeke and me.

There may be no finer meal that fresh sheep ribs cooked over a fire. The seared fat has a special flavor unique to the animal …. and to the circumstances. We had no trouble eating an entire rack of ribs. We'd had a wonderful day! Gorged bellies were a great way to end an experience like this one.

Our pack back to the cabin was leisurely and uneventful. It was fifteen degrees cooler and the bugs were few. No longer having a need to watch for our quarry, we made better time, even with the load, and we were more than half way home by the end of the first day. The other rack of ribs, along with some hot oatmeal and some dog food for Zeke, made a second fine supper.

About file miles from the cabin, it began to rain. The creeks all began to rise rapidly, but I was thankful that was coming then, rather than three or four days earlier. The cabin was dry and the Franklin stove soon took the damp chill off. I was thinking of some canned chili as I removed the gear and meat from the packboard, but my enthusiasm was dimmed when I found my cheapo camera had been mashed and was soaked with blood and water. I kept it in hopes of having at least one good photo of that huge ram, but the entire roll was ruined.

Rain and fog kept us cabin bound the next day which was a small price to pay for our unforgettable experience. We were back in Kotzebue with days to spare before the guest hunters arrived.

This was the second long sheep hunt I made with Zeke and it was his last. In December, 1979 he was hitched up and my wife, Mae, was racing

My best ram, an awful time to have a defective camera.

him with 11 of our huskies when another driver lost her team and ran into ours. A huge dog fight ensued and when the tangled teams split up Mae, was knocked off the sled and our team sprinted away. Zeke went down and never regained his footing. He was drug to death. Another racer caught our team and sent word to me that one of our dogs was down. I knew it had to be Zeke as soon as I heard that we'd lost one. It took Mae and I quite a while to get over that, but he loved racing nearly as much as hunting, and there are risks in both endeavors. The memories remain.

About a week after Zeke's death, Mae & I were home one bitterly cold evening when we heard a knock at the door. It was my two buddies, Dave and Fred, with another friend, Martha. I invited them in. I was feeling pretty low and I'm sure it showed. As they took off their coats, Fred said, "Hey Jake, come and feel Martha's chest." Mae and I looked at him and Martha, and was about to question that suggestion when I detected a small whimper from her direction. She opened up her coat to reveal a tiny black labrador puppy. I wasn't ready for that and tears fairly gushed from my eyes … and soon from my wife's and friends' eyes, too.

He was absolutely beautiful! I held him close to my nose and inhaled that slightly skunky lab puppy odor as he licked my face. Where did you find him, I stammered? We five adults were now laughing and trying not to cry.

Dave told me that another biologist friend, Woody, was in Anchorage and when he heard of Zeke's passing, he said he would try to find a pup to send up. There was a litter in town, but it was only five weeks old. The breeder didn't want to let any go so young, but Woody told him that he knew a man who needed that pup more than the pup needed it's mother. When Woody told the story of Zeke's death, the owner of the litter relented and sold him his pick of the litter.

Zeke had been the smallest male in his litter, which Woody knew, and he picked the smallest one for me. A super cub dog.

It's hard to try to describe the emotions of that evening, so I'll leave that to the reader's imagination.

We named the new pup "Max." He imprinted with Mae and me more thoroughly than any other dog I have ever known.

Soon I realized that I was blessed more richly than most men. Max was to become my second wonderful dog.

Fossil Rocks, or Sheep Huntin' Side Tracks

As I've often said, everything from earthworms to elephants is interesting to hunt, so it should be no surprise to anyone that occasionally, no... often... I get side tracked by other critters or even inanimate objects while engaged in the pursuit of the primary quarry.

Northwest Alaska has some very interesting fossil "beds". One summer I used both the wheel plane and the seaplane in taking food and supplies to a geologist, appropriately named Rock, who was out picking up samples destined for the assay lab when he returned to Fairbanks. He gathered bags of heavy minerals and stones which I took back to Kotzebue for safe keeping.

I guess one could say that I was helping him get his rocks off. But never mind that.

Already I was aware of fossil deposits in some locations and had accumulated an extensive, weighty collection of my own. Rock, the geologist, told me that the region had been thoroughly mapped and this information was available through the University.

He gave me a copy of a map which confirmed what I had independently discovered and much more. His map dated approximately when the fossils had been formed - give or take a few million years or so.

The areas I frequently hunted had, millions of years before, been covered by a warm coral sea. Continental shift and upthrust of plates - tectonic movements - had resulted in petrified coral heads appearing in sheep country, sometimes thousands of feet above the current sea level.

So, it was not unusual that I would add interesting rocks to my already heavy pack while hunting Dall sheep or other species of current times' local charismatic megafauna. To me an additional few pounds seemed worth the effort to carry some of the more impressive stones back to camp.

On a sheep hunt in 1973 I came across a very large coral head. This stream polished piece was an outstanding specimen. The ancient cotyledons showed distinctly, - their white color standing out in fine relief against the dark gray mother rock. However, the thing was more than two feet in length, fourteen inches thick and weighed over eighty pounds.

On the way up the mountain I made mental notes of the big coral's resting place, planning to return as soon as I could. That hunt was successful and as we returned to camp, loaded down with a ram, I intentionally passed again by that great piece of coral. I had it's location firmly committed to memory.

With several days left on the booking and the guest hunter complaining of sore legs and feet, the following day I left the guest in the tent and went back up the mountain alone for the coral head, - this time, with an empty pack. I only had a bit more than three miles to go.

It was not easy to get that danged thing into my pack, but I finally had it jammed in and secured - or so I thought. Unwieldy as it was, I started back down the mountain and was about a third of the way to camp, when my pack sack ripped open, dumping the fossil on my heels. Rats! Now I was crippled, for how long only time would tell, and in no way was I going to get that thing to the campsite that day. The only thing to do was make a good mental map of the rock's new residence and wait for another opportunity. I hobbled back to the camp with an ace bandage supporting one ankle, and I was now more lamed than my hunter.

As things developed, two years passed before I was again in that part of the Brooks Range.

On the next trip, I had two sheep hunters. I took them up past the great fossil, saying nothing to them about it, but verifying its location for my own sake. If they saw that rock, they might expect to have it for themselves, or perhaps a piece of it. I wanted it all and I was determined that eventually it would be mine.

At least that remarkable piece of ancient history was still lying unmolested in the same place. I had no opportunity to cart it any further that season.

The next August, five years to the day from my first sighting of that fossil, I was back with my surplus military pack board and plenty of rope. My lone sheep hunter for that week was happily making photographs of the pristine area, after collecting his ram. I had the whole day to move that

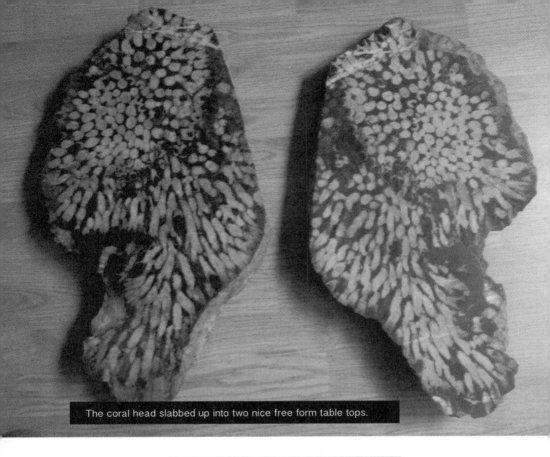

The coral head slabbed up into two nice free form table tops.

Next to my military packboard.

rock to our camp. I lashed it securely to the pack board and proceeded slowly toward the camp, taking care to not stumble or wrench my ankles or knees. This time the stone did not damage me. Once I got it hidden near the little brushy cub strip, I could make the hour long flight from Kotzebue to finally retrieve it whenever time and weather conditions permitted.

The day went well and by mid afternoon I had the great coral head secreted nearby and began to think of how I might cut it to display what I expected to be it's beautiful interior.

Patience is a virtue that sometimes eludes me, but it was necessary in regards to the fossil. Things came up and I had no time to return again that season.

The next summer I had charter work to do with the Bureau of Land Management in that same drainage. One of the BLM biologists needed to do a fish inventory on the stream that ran beside the crooked little brushy strip. I told him that I could land him there safely, but that we should keep our gear to a minimum as I had a stone that I needed to haul out. He agreed and was anxious to see the rock that had so captured my attention.

First we did the inventory, finding only some small sculpin of one to two inches in length and other smaller fish. After satisfying his survey, I took him to the coral head. He was impressed and asked if we might locate another, for him. After spending an hour looking in the stream bed, he decided that he would be too overloaded on his return home to carry such a rock, even if we found another one, which we did not do, so we gave up our discovery efforts. I carried my fossil the short distance to the strip, loaded it in the cub and departed. So, it took six years for me to get that one out.

In Kotzebue a friend with a large diamond saw cut the fossil in half and I was the proud owner of a matched set of unique coffee tables. Since then I have come across even larger fossil rocks, but that is the largest that I got all the way home.

Kodiak Island Provides Unique Opportunity for Trophy Deer

Over more than 40 years of hunting I had never seen a non-typical buck in the field, until 1994. In November of that year I glassed a two-point Sitka Blacktailed deer with antlers remarkable for their height, rather than spread. Closer scrutiny revealed the antlers to be extra heavy in the lower parts with a confusion of extra points clustered about the bases. With a strong wind blowing, this lone buck was browsing in a sheltered spot providing me with an easy approach. Before I squeezed off my shot I was surprised to see that both antlers were still carrying velvet. When I reached the downed deer I noticed that it had the body conformation of a doe, with a skinny neck and less developed shoulders than that of a normal rutting buck. Then I noticed that it seemed to have no testicles and that it lacked a scrotum, although it had a normal-looking penis. Although not the most impressive buck I had ever taken, it certainly was the most remarkable. I took several pictures of this unique deer. I remembered reading stories of similar "cactus bucks" occasionally taken in the lower forty-eight, sometimes described as having small atrophied scrotal testes.

I recalled from Zoology 101 that males without a scrotum or visible testes are termed a "bilateral cryptorchid". Bilateral means both sides (versus unilateral for one side) and cryptorchid means one or both testes remain in the abdominal cavity. Cryptorchidism results from faulty endocrine or RNA signaling, sometime between 25 and 40 days after fertilization, by genes involved in testicular descent.

Typically in these deer, the testes are found in the abdominal cavity midway between the kidneys and pelvis. Cryptorchid testes do not have a normal complement of germ cells and never produce spermatozoa; hence, a bilateral cryptorchid is sterile although a unilateral cryptorchid would be fertile. Cryptorchid testes do produce testosterone, although in reduced amounts, so a bilateral cryptorchid might shed velvet from newly grown antlers or show interest in mating.

Both unilateral and bilateral cryptorchids do shed their antlers annually.

Earlier that day in 1994 I had picked up a shed antler that was unusually heavy near the base and instead of a "button", it showed a concavity where the antler had detached from the skull. I had never seen such a shed before. This is common to sheds of bilaterally cryptorchid bucks, but not seen in every such case.

Non-typical antlers of the buck shot in November 1994.

Hunting in the same general area the following year I harvested three bucks still in the velvet in November that showed no testicles. In 1996, I took six such bucks. My curiosity aroused, I began asking Kodiak hunters about abnormal appearing bucks and heard of other velvet bucks occasionally taken from all areas of the island group. I deduced that these bucks must be cryptorchid, but several years passed before I found an undescended testis. After that, knowing what to look for, abdominal testes were easy to locate.

My partner and I were transporting deer sport hunters and each year an increasing percentage - up to 70% in some areas - of the deer harvested were bilateral cryptorchids. Some showed wildly non-typical antlers, some carried velvet, most had notably sharper antler tips, but some carried completely normal-appearing antlers.

It seems the whole gamut of antler types can be produced by bucks having this developmental abnormality. All these sterile bucks were very fat, averaging 8.5 years of age. Without going through the stress of rutting, the abnormal bucks seemed to have a much higher than average winter survival success.

We observed that most of the cryptorchids seemed more alert and spooky

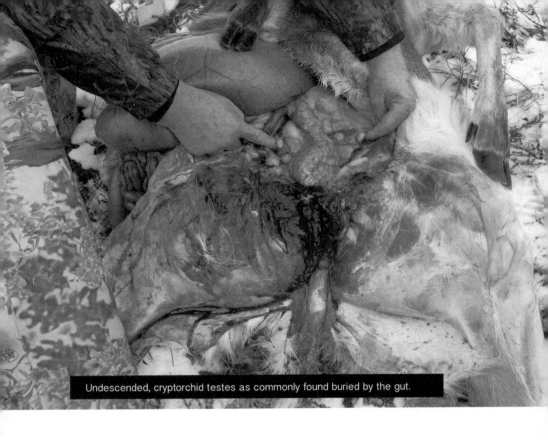

Undescended, cryptorchid testes as commonly found buried by the gut.

than normal deer of either sex. We harvested some normal-appearing bucks just after they completed mounting does, and found them to be bilateral cryptorchids, in spite of their rutting activities.

I guess they were shooting blanks.

In 1999 Dr. George Bubenik of the University of Guelph, Ontario agreed to analyze blood serum if I would collect and forward samples to him. The following year we co-authored the first of two research reports on these abnormal deer.

In 2002, Doctor Bubenik retired and in response to a short article in the Alaska Magazine, researchers at Colorado State University, specializing in male reproduction, learned of the problem and suggested that we collaborate to try to learn what was going wrong, despite the fact that we had very limited funds.

Having a life and living from hunting wild game, I saw it as good stewardship to pursue this strange phenomenon, so I provided time, effort and what funds I could afford to it.

The Colorado scientists analyzed my previously collected samples while I helped by gathering additional samples over several years. The reproduction scientists microscopically examined slices from the testes of many normal and cryptorchid males, and ran additional hormone analyses. As expected, abdominal testes lacked normal germ cells. Unexpected was the discovery that three types of carcinoma (cancer) were prevalent in abnormal testes, while rare in scrotal testes. The tentative conclusion was that an endocrine disruptor molecule, transferred from a recently impregnated doe to her developing embryos, likely was responsible for this unique situation. Lack of funding precluded identification on the toxic molecule(s).

Collaborative DNA analyses by geneticists at Purdue University led to exclusion of inbreeding as a cause. These research papers can be accessed via Google and typing "Sterile Sitka Blacktail Deer."

To establish the toxicant and path into the deer on southern Kodiak Island, substantial funding was needed.

With a field-research scientist from the University of Alaska, Anchorage, I traveled to Juneau in February 2008 with a proposal for a grant to be administered by the University to study this alarming situation. Legislators were courteous and receptive to our presentation, but Alaska Department of Fish and Game (ADF&G) officials strongly argued against funding.

Nevertheless, enlightening research is warranted for several reasons. Since transplantation to the Kodiak Islands in the 1920s, Sitka blacktailed deer have become an important food source, given that no native ungulates existed before. Subsistence hunters as well as sport hunters depend on deer for a large part of their annual diet. Sport hunting is a significant part of the local economy. Additionally, testicular cancer is increasing in humans (especially cryptorchid males) in all developed countries. The reason for this alarming increase in these types of cancers is unknown but similarities between the situation in men and Kodiak deer are striking. Might our wild Sitka deer be the classic "canary in a coal mine?"

Ethical considerations demand appropriate stewardship of our wild natural resources. The U.S. Fish and Wildlife Service (USF&W) has a Congressional mandate, a directive from D.C., to remove non-indigenous

Number 7 SCI non-typical Sitka Blacktail taken in 2009.

Number 2 SCI non-typical Sitka Blacktail taken in 2008.

species from lands they administer, as was done with the Hagemeister Island reindeer. USF&W does not seem to be actively pursuing removal of deer from Kodiak, but apparently they are unable, or unwilling, to engage in normal management of deer because the deer are not native to the area.

The ADF&G is charged with game management for sustained yield as its main mission. Yet, after nearly twenty years and multiple scientific publications and scores of anecdotal reports, the State of Alaska's response to increasingly widespread cryptorchidism in the Kodiak Archipelago has been to acknowledge that it occurs, ignore the problem, and discourage requests and efforts for research into possible causes and relationships.

How can this official stance can be justified?

It has been said that every cloud has a silver lining and hunters might see one in this case. Many of the cryptorchids grow very impressive head gear. Safari Club International recognizes nontypical Sitka Blacktail deer, including cryptorchids, and accepts them for entry in their record book. However, Boone and Crocket does not accept cryptorchid bucks for their official record book.

With the increase in frequency of abnormal Sitka deer, many new record book entries have been harvested in the Kodiak Archipelago in the last ten years, especially from the south end of the main island.

I encourage hunters to come to Kodiak to hunt deer which will provide a fine wilderness experience and some excellent table fare (ingestion of the meat is harmless). I urge all hunters to report the condition of antlers and the number of testicles found in the scrotum of their bucks to the ADF&G. It might prove worthwhile to contact Alaska Legislators on this issue. We need to thoroughly investigate this situation.

Joey's Buck

The past several years have been very good to me and my primary deer hunting partner, Rob Coyle, and 2010 proved to the third exceptional one in a row. In 2008, Rob took the new #2 SCI Non-typical Sitka Blacktail on a weekend hunt on the north end of the Kodiak Archipelago.

Amazingly, in 2009, Rob and I went to a new area, on a day hunt, and I found what measured out to be the new #7 buck in that category.

In 2010, Rob brought his 14 year old son, Joey, on an 8 day hunt with us. We would be using a tent. I've known Joey since he was small enough to be carried in his Dad's back pack as we pursued snowshoe hares and ducks. His enthusiasm for hunting, and everything else he does, has always been of the highest degree. Joey was bent on finding and harvesting a buck larger than his Dad's. Both Rob and I encouraged him. But the likelihood of even seeing such a buck was, ... well, not high. Nevertheless, Joey's boundless zeal and energy were inspirational for us all.

Privately I told Rob that if we sighted an exceptional buck, I hoped we could set Joey up to take it.

Rob replied, "I knew you would feel that way, Jake."

After setting up our camp, I walked to the beach to investigate an old Alutiiq midden site while Rob and Joey explored the country to the east. I returned just at dark and stirred up some supper, highlighted by ground venison burger from the 2009 season. When it was ready, I ate and laid down to read a bit.

About ten o'clock in the evening I woke up and wondered at the absence of my companions. But Rob is one of the most physically fit and level headed hunting partners I have ever had and I suppressed any thoughts of anxiety. We had seen no sign of bears and both my friends were adequately armed. I went back to sleep.

Shortly thereafter, I heard them coming.

That first day, Joey connected with a very good three point buck. (Western count, meaning the main beam, plus 2 points on each side, with brow tines to boot.) A nice neck shot at over 100 yards anchored his prize! That pleased us all, as Joey's previous best buck was a big two-by-two taken the previous year.

The buck fell at 7:00 pm - just before dark, but the hunters got it butchered, loaded on their packs and returned through the unfamiliar country slowly, using their head lights.

In the next few days, we all saw numerous "shooters" and Joey took another nice three pointer. His Dad and I each hung a buck on the meat pole, so we were all well satisfied with this wonderful hunt.

Joey Coyle with his #10 SCI Non typical Sitka Blacktail.

Weather beat us up some, keeping us tent bound due to heavy rain and wind for two days. It's a good idea to carry a book or two and a deck of cards on any Alaskan trip and we were thankful that we had done so. The fresh tenderloins and backstraps were a delicious addition to our menu.

As we calculated the weight limits for the DeHaviland Beaver which was due to pick us up and take us back to Kodiak, we had decided to limit our shooting to two bucks each, unless something really outstanding showed up.

Time was passing way too fast for us all, when on the next to last day, Rob downed another buck and as he and his son were prepping it for the packboard, Joey glassed a huge non-typical, still carrying velvet. He quickly brought that to his Dad's attention, but with more than a mile of rough, steep canyon terrane to negotiate, they wasted no time in covering the first kill to discourage birds and limit smell before they struck off for that extraordinary monster.

To learn more about Jake Jacobson's experience with cyptorchid bucks, read his previous hunt report titled, An Outstanding Sitka Blacktail "Cactus Buck." Jacobson has also co-authored a peer reviewed paper on cryptorchidism, which can be read here. In 2013 and future years Jake Jacobson will again conduct transported hunts for Sitka deer. through his outfit, Arctic Rivers Guide & Booking Service. Jacobson also made two hunt donations to the NRA for auction at the NRA Annual Meetings in Phoenix, Ariz., last May. He has been an NRA Life Member since 1976 and recently became a Patron Life Member.

Contact Information:

J.P. "Jake" Jacobson,
Alaska Master Guide #54

Arctic Rivers Guide
& Booking Service

P.O. Box 1313
Kodiak, AK 99615

486-5253
huntfish@ak.net
www.huntfish.us/

I'd collected a second buck to help fill our family's freezer and was back in camp well before dark when I heard Joey whoop as they walked in with his third trophy! The father and son had a quick sandwich, swallowed some mini candy bars, refilled their water bottles and charged back up the mountain to collect Rob's buck. Their day had begun early and it was nearly dark when they started back up for Rob's buck. Most grown men would dread another hike and carryout after a day like that, but in this area, if a deer is left overnight, not much, if anything will be left by morning. Bears, foxes, eagles, sea gulls and ravens all enjoy eating venison and are quick to find any available.

Joey never flinched at the prospect of two more hours of mountain walking and packing out meat.

More than half of the bucks we saw that November trip were still carrying velvet. In the Kodiak Archipelago that is one clear indication of the animal being cryptorchid, and therefore, sterile. This developmental abnormality has been increasing throughout the region since I harvested my first bilateral cryptorchid in 1994. About 30% of these bucks also show non typical antlers.

Since I was Joey's age, I have boiled and bleached most of my trophy heads and Joey wanted to prepare his in the European style also.

It's a little tricky to boil a head and not loose the velvet, especially if the buck was taken in August or September. The velvet of cryptorchids, however, is often retained until the antlers are shed. It is easier to maintain velvet in place during the skull boiling process, by wrapping the antlers with multiple layers of aluminum foil.

So Joey brought his big buck to my home to prepare. It turned out beautifully and that evening I scored it using the Safari Club International method.

As we totaled the numbers I told him that it was a super buck, but I didn't think it would make the top ten of the book.

Joey said "Yes it will, Jake!" He had reviewed the SCI site on the internet and knew his numbers. In fact, that buck is entered in the book as number ten.

Joey Coyle is off to a very good start as a hunter.

Bouy, that's a nice buck!

Odd things are often seen and done in pursuit of animals, proving that sometimes truth is indeed, stranger than fiction.

Several years ago we were hunting deer on the south end of Kodiak Island, where the deer are abundant and usually not so twitchy as those that have more frequent contact with humans.

On the "South End" alpine conditions exist from sea level to the highest hills, which are can be up to 2500 feet or so in elevation. My sister, Pat, and I were hunting together on a peninsula characterized by rolling hills and broad valleys with little vegetation other than alders of four to ten feet high growing along the streams. A few struggling clumps of willows grow here and there.

The ever tireless wind was blowing about 20 to 25 miles per hour, as is common for that area.

We'd left the beach about a mile and a half back, hunting along slowly, glassing constantly before we sat down to enjoy our lunch and a drink of water when one of the guest hunters from our boat appeared below us. He looked up and joined us. This fellow, who I will call Lawrence, said he'd seen a good number of deer, of which about fifty percent were bucks, but none carried antlers with more than two points per side. I told him that was typically what one could expect, but a little time and patience would no doubt lead him to a better buck.

He pulled out his sandwich and sat down, joining us for lunch.

As we were preparing to walk on, Pat, with her binoculars stuck to her face announced that she'd just seen a buck stand up in an alder patch across the valley and he looked pretty good. A quick look with my "long eyes" revealed his rack to have three long points on each side with what

The "bouyed buck".

appeared to be velvet remaining on the right antler. It was the best buck we'd seen that day.

Lawrence was giving the situation his full attention, but could not locate the deer. As I was trying to describe its location, the deer seemed to make a little struggle, then lunged forward at which time an orange colored thing near his flank became visible. By the color, I knew immediately that it had to be a rubber fishing bouy. It was rutting time and bucks often decide to attack inanimate objects, but this was a new experience for me, probably for the deer, also.

Lawrence was becoming frustrated in his attempts to locate the deer, so I said that he should just look next to the big orange in the alder patch. That allowed him to zero in and he was impressed with the trophy.

Lawrence's brother, Carl caught up to us, so I suggested that they get after that buck and not to worry, as I had captured it the night before and bouyed it to make it easy to find and to slow it down.

Pat and I went a different direction and soon heard some shots. About an hour later as we were headed back to the beach we went by the area and found the brothers admiring the fine buck. Apparently the bouy had washed up on a beach, with a piece of line attached. When the rutty buck attacked the bouy, the line became entangled in its antlers and the unfortunate beast had been burdened with this unnatural parasite ever since. We were about a mile and a half from the nearest beach and deer seldom walk in straight lines, so it must have been dragging and fussing with that bouy for several miles. It was a lucky thing that a bear had not found it before we did.

Pat and I had each harvested a buck and we sat down to rest with our loads as the brothers butchered the deer and soon were putting their meat into their packs. I was using hand loaded Nosler 150 grain Ballistic Tip bullets and happened to drop one from my pocket. Lawrence noticed the green plastic tip and asked what that was. I told him that was a "meat seeker" tip. His eyebrows raised, questioning, and I said that a mini computer in the tip was designed to be drawn to heat and it made shooting much more effective. My sister kept her silence as the brothers just stared at me.

Coupled with the bouyed buck, my special bullets had Lawrence and Carl showing signs of profound contemplation, but they never did question me on either issue.

Boddington's Best Buck

In the 1980s I had the pleasure of Craig Boddington's company on some hunts for Coes deer in Arizona. We got on well and he recommended me for a speaking job with the Shooting and Hunting Sports Fair which was a lot of fun and productive for me in booking guests for Alaska.

My tales of hunting Sitka Blacktail Deer in the Kodiak Archipelago piqued Craig's interest and we planned to pursue those critters together in early November, 1992.

I had no booked hunters for November and often in such situations invite a friend to join me on my annual meat hunt. Of course while meat hunting we all keep an eye out for trophy bucks, as well.

The boat I had arranged to take us on the trip was not yet in Kodiak when Craig arrived. I saw an opportunity for a good laugh, so rather than tell him right off, I picked him up at the airport and drove him to the harbor. We carried his bags and rifle down one of the floats to a decrepit looking old wooden tub named the *Leprechaun*. It was a 32 footer with no inside controls and not even a single porthole.

The ancient bark had long since slipped from any semblance of customer appeal, to say the least. Long green moss hung from the hull. Seagulls had used it as a perch and poop depository to such an extent that in some places, their droppings resembled piles of bat guano. Oil oozed from the old hulk, giving a purple sheen to the water that partially supported its tonnage. I believe it was the most unseaworthy appearing craft in the harbor.

I had chosen it carefully.

I jumped from the walkway onto the deck of the *Leprechaun* and told Craig to hand me his bags.

Boddington's expression could only be described as one of abject horror.

"We,... we... we're not going to go out on THAT, are we, Jake?"

"Craig, you impossible landlubber! You really don't know boats do you? Why, this proud ship has been around Kodiak so long, it doesn't even need a skipper. Just crank the engine, turn 'er loose and we'll be off. It's better than an automatic pilot for sure," was my reply.

I wrenched Craig's bag from him and plopped it on the hatch cover, then extended my hand to help him aboard. By reflex he grabbed my hand and found himself on the boat, the deck of which was creaking from the addition of our weight.

Ever courteous, Craig asked if I had been on the boat before. I said, "Not till now, Craig, but I've longed for the opportunity ever since I first laid eyes on her. She has a well known reputation. She's truly one of the most talked about of the Kodiak 'girls'". I could no longer hold it and soon was in spasms of laughter.

He muttered something about me being such a s--t, or some such thing, then joined me in laughter, tinged with nervous relief.

Of possible interest to the reader, the *Leprechaun* sank in its slip two months later.

We got out of port the next day on the scheduled boat, bound for the South End of Kodiak. As a vendor for the State of Alaska, I had plenty of deer tags available, but suggested to Craig that he purchase them one at a time, as to do otherwise is tempting fate, even in the best deer hunting place in the world. He agreed. We need not tempt Murphy...or fate.

Our journey was complete after 16 hours of continuous running. The next morning we cruised offshore, glassing the hillsides and beaches. With little snow, the deer were still high. Craig and I got dropped on a beach by the skiff man, who told me he was planning to return to pick us up before dark.

Boddington, then a Colonel in the Marine Reserves, (he was selected for promotion to Brigadier General in 2001) was in top shape and he likes to walk, as do I.

We covered a lot of country on foot. It was cold enough that we found only a few occasions to sit and glass for more than a few minutes. When we spotted the first buck that he liked, it required holding tight for more than half an hour. In the cold wind, Craig was soon doing push ups to regain body heat.

Craig Boddington checking out the Leprechaun.

Craig had brought a rifle chambered in .35 Whelen, but with the ranges we found it necessary to shoot, he used my .300 Winchester Magnum for all three of his bucks. He shoots left handed, but had no problem with my factory rifle built for right handers.

His first buck was a handsome 3X3 with brow tines and an estimated live weight of 235 pounds. It was a very good Sitka Blacktail.

We had a full week to hunt and the year before I had taken a Boone and Crockett Sitka buck in that area, so we covered a lot of ground, looking for an exceptional one.

Toward the end of day five, Craig had a beautiful red fox in his pack. We'd been seeing up to 100 deer per day, but had not found a monster male. He decided to settle on a very good 3X4 and dispatched it with one shot from my rifle.

He said, "Jake, that's enough for me. You want to hunt, too, so tomorrow we'll concentrate on your end of things.

That night on the boat, as I skinned the fox, I convinced him to buy a third tag to carry on the last day.

Soon after being put ashore we jumped a huge buck at sixty yards that took off quartering away to the right. I told him to take it and Craig leveled off with the Whelen and fired.

I said, "You missed him, Craig!"

"What?", he said in a voice two octaves above his normal tone.

There was no time for a second shot. The buck was over the ridge and out of sight following a huge bodied doe.

We both remarked on what a huge buck that was and it was carrying the largest rack we had seen the entire week. I told him that we were going to stay with that deer and get him, as we had a good six hours before having to be back on the beach.

A quick run took us to the ridge and we began scrutinizing the country with binoculars. Soon, we spotted the buck, accompanied by that extraordinarily large doe.

Boddington's First Sitka Buck.

We continued behind them, loosing them several times due to terrane contours, then relocating them most often by recognizing that giant doe, then glassing in the area near her.

After more than three hours in pursuit, we rounded a hill and seemed to have lost the deer. Persistent glassing revealed that huge doe standing in long grass, browsing on ferns. After a few minutes, I was able to identify one antler of the buck, which was lying down. Not sure it was the right one, we continued to watch until the doe ambled further away. This brought the buck to his feet and, indeed, it was "the" one.

We edged as close as we could, not wanting to spook them again. The doe came back our way and the buck soon laid down. At about 300 yards, with only the head visible, Craig laid on the tundra and squeezed off a shot. The buck disappeared. The shot was true and I got it on video.

We got to the buck in what seemed like no time and were open mouthed impressed! It was as big a Sitka buck, both in body size and antler dimensions, as I had ever seen!

Boddington's Best Sitka Buck. Huge body, too!

Boddington's Second Sitka Buck and a Fox

Shortly after reaching the buck, a large, dark Brown bear appeared on the ridge above us. Craig's one shot was all it took for that top predator to home in on us. This bear, like most big, old Kodiak bruins, patiently sat on his rump as we hurried to butcher and load the deer. As we left the site, the old fellow sauntered down to slurp up the innards.

"Jake, this is the buck of a lifetime. Fabulous. You know, I've been able to do a lot of deer hunting here and there, but I believe this is probably the best quality deer of any that I have," Craig told me.

I have Craig as he said this on my website: www.huntfish.us/

Twenty years later in magazine articles and books, Craig still lauds that buck as his best.

Craig has all the qualities I value in a guest. He is thoughtful, polite, very fit and doesn't take himself too seriously. I've hunted with other writers, but never with one that was such pleasurable company as Craig Boddington.

He wrote a story of our hunt titled "THE BEST DEER HUNTING IN THE WORLD" for the September, 1993 Petersen's Hunting magazine. The title tells it all.

In 2004, in his book FAIR CHASE IN NORTH AMERICA, Craig relates the story of our hunt and says that "To date he (the big buck) is my finest North American deer, and one of my most memorable shots."

All hunts and guests should be so pleasurable.

Getting White Fish for Winter Dog Food

In 1970 my wife, Mae, suggested that we get a few sled dogs. Even a three dog team could provide transportation for us to and from the post office and grocery store in winter. Plus we could avoid the frustrations inherent with snow machines of that era. It sounded like a good idea to me. Within two years, however, our dog lot held 32 adult huskies. Somehow, the three dog team had grown.

Feeding the dogs was time consuming, but we never thought of it as being onerous. We had scraps from hunting and fishing, and as we enjoyed those activities, the dogs gave us reason to do even more. We supplemented natural foods with store bought dog pellets, but the dogs seemed to do best on meat and fish from the country. Seal and beaver meat were favored.

Several local old timers were generous with advice and assistance. One fellow in particular, Doc Harris, was a great help to us. One fall he asked how we were getting fish for our dogs and how we prepared the dog food. I told him that we saved carcasses from fish that we'd filleted, we put winter caught fish in our cache and let the outside temperatures do the rest.

Doc asked if I would like to take part in catching and putting up fish for dogs, the Eskimo way. I said that I surely would like to do that. He said he could show me how it was done.

The following week I flew him in the super cub looking for an opportunity. Soon we found that the lagoon on Cape Krusenstern would be perfect.

The long, narrow drainage of that lagoon had been blocked by pea gravel washed in by waves of a southern storm. Its normal outlet had been completely closed. From the air we could see Whitefish of several species that had collected in great numbers near the outlet as they attempted their seasonal migration to the bay. The lagoon had been blocked for about a week and the outbound flow of fish seeking the salt water would likely last for another two weeks or more, he said. Doc suggested that we could "fool those fishes" and easily get lots of winter food for our dogs. There were clouds of fish ready to run to the sea.

I took Doc back to Kotzebue and he said that in about three days his family would be at the lagoon and we could go back with the airplane, land on the beach and get at working on catching the fish.

Weather held favorable for us and three days later I took him back to see that his family's two boats were on the beach, a wall tent was erected and people were busy digging to clear the blocked channel, preparing the trap.

The beach was composed of soft pea gravel but had only a gentle rise from the water to the grass. It provided easy access to the area for a light airplane, but I gently touched the main gear down and ran a ways under power to be sure it was not too soft. When I made the full stop landing, I kept my heels off of the brakes to avoid nosing up and we enjoyed a safe, smooth landing.

The technique was to clear the channel downstream from the lagoon for about twenty to forty yards, but not all the way to the salt water. A small "bridge" was left at the lower end of the lagoon. When holding pits had been dug near the end of the re-trenched channel and everyone was ready, the "bridge" was dug out and the outrush of water brought hundreds of fish along with it. When the surge of water and fish hit the end of the channel, the water disappeared into the gravel and the fish were left stranded and flopping. They were easily scooped up by hand or shovels and placed into a nearby grass lined holding pit.

As long as a little current led down the channel, the fish kept coming, thinking they were bound for the open sea. When the current slowed too much or stopped, the process was repeated, leap frogging about twenty yards at a time until the fishermen had enough fish or the fish quit coming. If fish were still plentiful, but the channel approached too close to the bay, a gravel dam could be placed again at the natural drainage of the lagoon, bridges shoveled back in place at twenty yard intervals and in a few days, or however long it took for the build-up of fish to warrant it, the process was repeated. After being "caught" the fish were thrown into the holding pits without gutting. "Feathers and all", as Grandma used to say. If the ambient

Lagoon with an ideal outlet, at the far end.

When the outlet is opened, fish go with the current and beach themselves.

A ton of fresh whitefish in one of several holding pits.

temperature was not low enough to immediately freeze the catch, a slight "ripening" of the flesh took place. Doc said the dogs always preferred their fish to be "a little bit ripe".

The efficiency and simplicity of this method of fishing impressed me. I made a few photographs of the operation and returned to town the next day with Doc and a few sacks of fish. His family stayed on for over a week, securing enough fish for their needs and ours with some extra to sell or trade.

Transporting the catch required multiple trips back to Kotzebue in the two boats.

All in all, it was a very satisfactory and economically efficient means of putting up a winter's supply of fish.

Snowshoe Hares

Hares are born fully furred and with eyes open, while rabbits are born blind and hairless.

During my first year in Alaska, 1967, I got into hunting Snowshoe or Varying hares (Lepus americanus) on several occasions, from Kodiak Island to the Matanuska Valley and then the North West Arctic. In most places they were scarce, so my shotgun was the weapon of choice.

These smaller hares, which weigh three to five pounds and are indigenous to mainland Alaska, had been introduced to Kodiak and Afognak Islands by a transplant of 558 hares which were captured along the Alaska Railroad near Anchorage in 1934 by the Alaska Game Commission. That was one of several new game species introductions done during Territorial times. Today such an introduction would never be allowed by the EPA and other regulatory agencies.

Thank goodness the old Alaskan's got it done! Their hare introduction filled a vacant nitche and were a rich addition to the nutrition and sport of the Archipelago. Subsequent captures on Kodiak Island allowed introduction of these animals to Long and Woody Island. Today, snowshoe hares are found from the northern extremes to the south end of the Archipelago.

In 1970, using shotguns on the lower Noatak River, just north of Kotzebue, myself and a friend would think it a good day if we came home with four hares each. The population increased dramatically and the next year we were using .22 rifles and harvesting a dozen. The following year, it was common to bring home twenty hares each.

This was great fun during the heavy snow conditions of winter and spring. I could travel by small plane, dog team or snow machine twelve to fifteen minutes north of town to the Little Noatak Slough. With my labrador retriever, I could, in a couple of hours, have several pounds of highly nutritious food, as well as great exercise and wonderful memories. Our neighbors were happy to get a share, as were our huskies.

Occasionally in March or April I would take one of our dog teams out for a few days away from town. I carried frozen or half dried fish (usually several species of whitefish) and other types of dog food - and always some picture hanging wire for snaring hares. The snares worked very well, especially in times or areas of less abundance of bunnies. Once the hare population got high, it was easier to just shoot as many as we needed.

I fed hares to the dogs intact, "feathers and all," and when a dog had diarrhea, feeding it a whole hare seemed to cure the trots. I kept a .22 rifle and a larger caliber firearm in scabbards on the sled on those trips which sometimes resulted in a Caribou, Wolf, Wolverine or Lynx to take home with us as a bonus.

One November a fellow flew up from Seattle to hunt the fabled Snowshoe Hare with me. I took him on the short flight to the Little Noatak and as we were putting our snowshoes on, he commented on how wonderful and wild the place was, in spite of it being only minutes away from town. That year the slough, as well as the bay north of Kotzebue, had frozen absolutely flat and most of the snow had blown off, leaving clear ice. A grader had made a good ice road from Kotzebue to the Kobuk River villages. That road passed near the mouth of the slough making that area also accessible to vehicular traffic. It was a rare condition. The guest had no more than expressed his wonderment at the awesomely pristine location when a taxi cab came around the corner with occupants leaning out the windows, rifles at the ready for hares or whatever might present itself. Once again, it seemed, Murphy had been listening. Never before or since have I seen a taxi cab in that area. The cab somewhat diminished my guest's wonder at the wilderness.

In the late 1970s, the snowshoe hare population was so high that some of the older growth willows were being girdled by feeding hares, causing the plants to die. I wondered if the hares might become a threat to moose by over feeding and killing willows. Then I read a peer review article written by a Canadian biologist that made a case for willows that were about to be girdled, emitting a chemical noxious to hares. I disparaged that and referred to it as "Revenge of the Plants", but after reading similar pieces, I began to believe it.

1981 Jake with 11 dog team, Lower Noatak River

An afternoon hunt on the Noatak Slough in March, 1980.

My daughter, Bess, with a snowshoe hare at our hunting lodge, in the NW Arctic. 2009.

Sept. 2010 Bob Sirna, with Snowshoe Hares.

I began to carefully check the bigger willows and never did find one completely girdled by hares.

By the winter of 1979/1980 the Snowshoe Hare population was at it's peak. On a good afternoon, with the assistance of my labrador, Max, I could take up to 200 hares in an afternoon using a .22 rifle. With thirty-two adult huskies to feed, neighbors to treat and our own appetites, none of the harvested hares went to waste.

In April, 1980 I noticed that the hares were showing an increasing frequency of bloody diarrhea. The following winter we did not find much sign of hares. I did not see another hare at our lodge on Trail Creek until 2005. I had read that Varying Hares cycle from high to low numbers about every seven years. This cycle had taken much longer than most - it was a full 25 years.

After the big die-off, I would notice a few tracks here and there. Hares in that area normally produce two or three litters each year, with one to eight young per litter. Recruitment can be phenomenal under even marginal conditions. Why it took so long for the population to reach huntable numbers remains an unexplained mystery to me.

With steady increases in the population beginning in 2005, by 2009 we would commonly see six or eight hares at a time from the windows of the lodge.

So, once again, "Northern Fried Rabbit" has become a frequent meal for us, as well as a fine way to spend an evening pursuit near the lodge after a day of big game hunting.

In 2010 we had lynx at the lodge for the first time since 1980. The Red Fox and Arctic Fox populations proliferated as well in that area, 167 miles above the Arctic Circle.

On only two occasions in my 44 years of hunting in Alaska have I seen Wolves in active pursuit of lemmings or other small rodents. It seems that the economics of metabolic effort versus nutritional gain for Wolves hunting small rodents is not advantageous. However, I have often seen evidence of Wolves devouring Snowshoe Hares and believe that is common, especially in times of scarcity of big game such as Caribou and Moose.

It is a real blessing to once again have an abundance of Hares in the areas I hunt. I hope it lasts a long time.

Published in the *Better Beagling,* December 2011.

Arctic Hares

I'd heard lots of stories about Arctic Hares, (Lepus Arcticus). The Alaskan subspecies are often called Alaskan Hare (Lepus othus). The big jackrabbits are found here and there throughout Alaska, with large empty spaces in between the known populations of these lagomorphs.

Like the more common Snowshoe or Varying Hare, Lepus Americanus, these food animals breed prolifically, bearing multiple litters in most years with three to eight young in each litter. With a gestation period of about a month, sexual maturity at six months, and a life span of up to eight years, Alaska's two species of wild hares play a crucial role in the life cycles (i.e. food chain) of other species such as foxes, lynx and humans. The young of these prolific critters are called leverets and can walk as soon as their hair is dry after birth which takes place in an unlined depression called a "form". In a day or two they walk around near the "nest" and are eating greens. They nurse for only about a month.

Arctic Hares have black tips on their ears, but their body hair is white all the way to the base. Compared to snowshoe hares, their leather is thicker, their fur is warmer and their larger size makes them highly desirable as items of clothing, for which they are still used in some areas.

Arctic Hares seem to prefer more open, windswept areas and dig through snow cover to reach various plants of the tundra.

Unlike the more independent Snowshoe Hare, the Arctic Hare is a seasonally gregarious animal, found during early springtime in groups sometimes numbering in the hundreds. Also unlike the smaller hare, which in many areas overpopulates, then crashes, followed by gradual rebuilding of the population, the Arctic Hare numbers remain relatively stable, without huge crashes.

My friend Bill Munz, a well known Arctic aviator and gold miner told me that once he was flying over sea ice between Little Diomede Island and Cape Prince of Wales, when he noticed what he initially surmised to be blowing snow beneath him. Upon closer scrutiny, the surface was literally alive with Arctic Hares, all moving toward shore. I had never seen such a huge collection of hares and was fascinated with the story.

Eskimos living on Seward Peninsula had told me that the big hares gather for breeding in March and are often seen in company with both Arctic and Red Foxes. The adult hares are larger than Arctic Foxes and seemed to pay no heed to either specie of fox during the gathering time in March and April.

I had harvested single Arctic Hares on a few occasions, primarily during spring Grizzly bear hunts and found most females to have five to nine developing embryos. These hares were solitary and seemed more twitchy and harder to stalk than their smaller cousins, the Snowshoe Hares.

But I had never encountered one of the storied "herds" of the big ones. One sunny day as I was flying back to Kotzebue from a trip to Wales village, I cut across Cape Espenberg to take a look at the Goodhope River country.

On the open hillsides I saw what appeared to be caribou feeding craters in the snow. As Caribou did not frequent this area, I slowed down, dropped the flaps and circled back for a closer inspection. I saw hundreds of Arctic Hares! I had skis on the super cub, so I landed on a small frozen lake and using my 25:06 with solid bullets, shot two of the big bunnies.

My family and I relished the meat of hares, as did our 32 adult huskies. These big ones tasted even better than the 3 to 4 pound snowshoe bunnies. After sampling them in the home kitchen, I resolved to return to the Goodhope River for more, before they dispersed. The meat was a motivator in this, but even more important, I just wanted to observe this remarkable collection of animals. It was another natural wonder to investigate and appreciate.

During the next two weeks I made time for two more trips to the Goodhope River and each time found that huge collection of hares. These animals did not seem to gnaw the bark of the willows so much as the snowshoe hares do, preferring to dig through the snow to browse the sedges, lichens and other tundra flora. My .22 magnum was ideal for taking them.

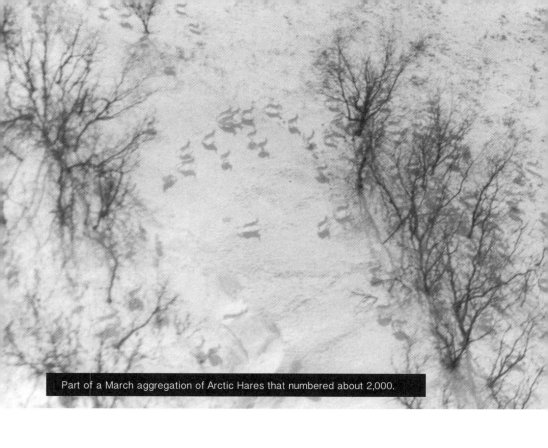

Part of a March aggregation of Arctic Hares that numbered about 2,000.

Max and I with 13 Arctic Hares on the Goodhope River.

Once leaving the super cub I was afoot, often on snowshoes, and soon found that four bunnies was a comfortable load to carry back to the plane. Then I would go back for more. A load of a dozen or so of these delicious beasts made a two hour aircraft flight worthwhile.

When in huge aggregations, Arctic Hares seem less wary and they made for easier hunting than later in the spring when they have dispersed and once again are solitary.

At three to four times the weight of our smaller Snowshoe Hares, my 40 pound Labrador struggled a bit with his retrieval work, but he clearly loved every bit of it.

True to the stories, I'd heard, I saw both Arctic Fox and Red Foxes in close proximity to the big hares, sometimes running together with no concern being shown by the hares.

I had been told by some local old timers that most Arctic Hares would tip the scales at 25 pounds, but after weighing several of the largest ones that spring, the heaviest was just a bit over 17 pounds.

Once frozen with the skin on, it takes longer to thaw out an Arctic Hare than it does to thaw an Arctic or Red Fox for skinning.

I suppose their diets may explain the difference in taste of the two types of hares found in Alaska. Both are delectable, the bigger ones are just a bit better.

Published in the *Better Beagling*, April 2011.

Epiphany on Kodiak

November, 2005 was notable for early, heavy snow and generally lousy weather on the southeast end of Kodiak Island. Snow drifts were over knee deep in places and drifts on the lee side of the prevailing North West winds were too deep to gauge.

We had a group of 4 Veterinarians from Arizona, New Mexico and California down for a week of deer hunting. These fellows were all really interested in the cryptorchidism which we found to be so prevalent amongst the bucks, particularly in the "hot zone" were we'd taken them. I was pleased to have such experienced professionals along to help me with my sampling of tissues, and especially to educate me on what to expect from and how to handle ovaries. I'd decided to collect a few does, to see if any sign of fertility abnormalities might show up in the female population, as well as the males.

The first day out, walking through the hummocky terrane, I'd fallen forward several times, twisting both of my knees. Over the years, I've done considerable damage to my joints, most of all to my knees. This time, they never fully recovered and in early March, 2007 I had both surgically replaced.

The heavy snow had resulted in deer moving closer to the beaches and by now, about 10 days since the biggest snowfall, they were bunched up. Some groups had dozens of deer, some mobs numbered in the hundreds.

Anyway, the Transported guest hunters were all out doing their thing, so I took a route not traveled by any of them and soon saw a group of about 60 deer traveling cross wind along the face of some rounded hills about a mile inland from the beach. The wind was blowing from twenty-five to forty miles per hour offshore - right in my face. I headed straight toward the group of deer I had sighted and saw a large antlered, normal appearing 3X3 buck hanging near the tail end of the bunch. He was acting like he was heavily into the rut and I saw him mount a doe, so, with no one on the boat having collected testes from any normal bucks so far, I was determined to harvest that one. The deer study needed some normal bucks as control samples.

As I progressed toward the deer I crossed a huge, very fresh bear trail. And I mean trail, not just tracks. The snow was deep enough and the bear's belly so pendulous that he left a trail that looked like a broad drag mark punctuated by deep lateral indentations made by his feet, or maybe a railroad train. The trail was left by a very big bear in deep snow.

After not too much maneuvering I got an opportunity to shoot that buck on a ridge that I was familiar with and knew provided a clear field of view in all directions. A military description would be a "field of fire" - a good spot to drop a deer in bear country. I shot once and the deer dropped out of sight. When I got up on the ridge, I found hair, but no deer. The bullet had struck him high, at the top of the spinous processes of his neck, which dropped him immediately, but he'd tumbled down a steep incline, then recovered. I saw him running at the back of the bunch of deer in the stream bed below. This time I led him a bit and made a heart shot. On impact, he ran for about a 50 yard spurt and dropped.

Another 15 minutes and I was standing over the buck. He was indeed a normal buck with 2 scrotal testes, but with the certainty of a bear nearby, this location was far from ideal. I could drag the deer about 40 yards downwind, giving me that distance from the alders along the stream, but that would put me at the base of a steep hill. With the wind blowing from the base to the top of that hill, any bear downwind would naturally approach me and the dead deer from the top of the hill, about 40 yards uphill from where I would be butchering the buck. That was not a cheery or attractive prospect.

The deer had collapsed about 15 yards from an alder patch to the East and 10 yards from a thicket to the North. To the west, I would stand with my back against alders. I decided to quickly take the RNA, blood and tissue samples on the spot, then cut up the deer and tie the four quarters, back straps and ribs onto my pack board. Under ideal conditions, I've been clocked at 17 minutes for that procedure. I put the wiggle on for this one.

I drew the 2 tubes of blood, processed the gubernaculum and teste slices for RNA, took liver and other tissue pieces and put all samples in their respective vials or bags. Soon, I had the 2 hindquarters and one front tied onto the pack board. I was continually looking up and around for the bear.

I was more than just a little bit twitchy, mind you. As I began to tie on the second front quarter, I looked up again to gaze into the stare of a huge bear, not 15 yards away on a small piece of ground to the east of me. I've often heard that the most common thing people say in a tight situation is "Shit". But what came out of my mouth was "GOD"! (I guess that subliminally I was expecting to be finally judged by Him soon!) Then I was yelling "NO, No, No". All the vocalizations were spontaneous and involuntary, as I grabbed my rifle, stuck in the snow at arm's reach. I jacked a round into the chamber, still vocally stuck on "NO, No, No". I really felt like this was "my time" and that bear was soon going to be beating me up, but I was resolved to not be passive about it.

After our initial gaze at each other, the bear never again made eye contact with me, but he came striding down the incline toward me and the dead deer. I decided that if he looked at me, I would brain him, as no other shot placement would stop a beast of that size at such close range.

I was still stuck on "NO, NO, NO…" when the bear got to the deer guts and carnage, but he paused very briefly and then turned away, with me still hollering "NO, No, No…" That bear didn't even pick up a piece of guts or anything. I think he was a bit surprised and confused.

Just before he turned away, he was so close that I could have leaned forward, reached out and touched his left flank. He passed maybe 5 feet away from me.

The bear slowly walked away, getting behind the alders to the north, then at about thirty yards away, it turned to look my way and began to pop its jaws, making a sound like clapping of one's hands in applause, but his were single, deliberate percussions.

I interpreted this to mean that the bear was wanting me to get out of there and I was happy to be able to comply. I put my pack board on, with some tie lines trailing loose, grabbed my bag of samples in my left hand with my rifle in my right hand and began to back up.

I tripped and fell backward, and remembering that my chamber was loaded and the safety was not on, I thought how bad it would be to shoot my own foot off. I put the safety on, looked downwind and backed to the base of the bluff, concentrating my gaze on the patch of brown fur making noises behind the alders.

The bear then walked forward to stand at the gut pile, seemingly oblivious to me. I realized that in the exigency, I had lost my reader glasses, but to heck with that, he could have 'em.

I went up the hill, alternating glances in the area I was headed with looks back at the bear enjoying the remains of the deer. In addition to the guts, he got one front quarter and the ribs,...and my glasses, but that was ok.

When I returned to the beach to meet the skiff that would take us back to the big boat, I had some time to just sit and think over my experiences of the day. I guess I went into meditation mode. By 2005, after literally hundreds of bear encounters over my then 39 years of hunting in Alaska, I'd seen a lot of bears up close - but never that close before. That bear appeared to be a huge old boar. We only made eye contact at the time of my initial sighting of him, at very close range. The bear never did give an appearance of aggression.

I had shot 2 times at the deer. The bear had been upwind and probably a quarter of a mile away. My second shot had been from about 200 yards and uphill from the spot where the deer dropped, but that bear had homed right in on me and the dead deer. That's all pretty amazing, as the bear could not have smelled us, or seen us until the initial encounter.

His demeanor was more matter of fact, deliberate, but not determined - if that makes sense to anyone reading this.

If future circumstances should put me in position to do so, I would choose to not shoot that old bear. He was of a nature to be revered, to my way of thinking. A good bear.

That evening I mentioned my encounter to the others and suggested that if they saw a big bear wearing a pair of reader glasses, I hoped they would not shoot it.

The following week, Spencer, my oldest grandson had come down from Kotzebue for a hunt. He and I revisited the site and measured the distance between the little knoll the bear had been on and where the gut pile and I were. It was just under fifteen yards. New snow had removed all sign of the previous weeks' activities, but I sensed the aura of that unique experience...and that great bear.

Tracks of the Big Kodiak Brown Bear that was less than 5 feet from me.

About 3 weeks later I saw that same bear under similar, but less threatening circumstances. We had dropped two guest hunters off on the beach, with several deer showing on the bluff just above. A friend and field research biologist from the University of Alaska, Loren Buck, was with me. We saw two of the hunters heading toward the deer, so we continued into the hills well away from them, to avoid spooking their quarry. The wind was once again blowing offshore at about 25-35 mph.

When we were a half mile from the beach we heard several shots from the guest hunters. We continued on, glassing the hills upwind from us. In about five minutes I spotted the big bear as he topped a ridge, more than 1,000 yards away, headed right for the sound of the shots. He had heard the shooting from more than a half mile away, in spite of the wind, and was moving rapidly toward the hunters. I remarked to Loren, "That bear's on a mission. I'll bet we'll be hearing some shouts and shots from those two hunters soon. Sure hope they don't wind up shooting that gentleman bear."

In a couple of minutes we did hear some frantic shouting and then two shots. We were up on the foothills and could glass the hunters and the bear. The bruin had laid down about 60 yards from the men, who were by then dragging their deer toward the beach. As they disappeared over the bluff, the old bear moved in to slurp up the guts. An admirably well mannered bear.

I'd seen this sort of behavior displayed by big bears in that area before, but never had I observed such remarkable navigation as this. To have heard the shots from so far upwind and then, without sighting or smelling the men, home directly to the site, still amazes me.

Loren and I got to the beach, each with samples and meat of a buck on our pack boards and got the story from the hunters. I'd cautioned them to keep a sharp eye out for bears and they were doing just that when the older fellow saw the bear coming. The two of them began yelling and waving their hats, then they shot in front of the approaching bear. In my experience, both in the Arctic with interior Grizzlies and with Kodiak bears, shooting like that seldom will stop a bear's advance, but this one did stop and then laid down until the hunters had departed with the buck.

Well, I wish that old beach master well and hope that somehow his behavior has been genetically passed on to future bruins of the area.

Meeting Fred Machetanz

In August, 1970 I was once again Assistant Guiding for Jim Cann in Skolai Pass. Things were going well and our first two sheep hunters had scored with a few days left in their booking. They decided to go home early and Jim planned to use the time to go back to Anchorage for some supplies and other business. I stayed in camp.

The weather was perfect for hunting, as one might expect for a period of time with no hunters in camp. Murphy never rests, it seems. I enjoyed the days shooting ptarmigan for fresh meat, digging a new latrine, making some short scouting trips and reading.

One afternoon I crawled into my bag for a nap when I heard a helicopter, so I got up to see what it was doing.

Days before a band of about thirty ewes and lambs had moved in across the Pass from our tents. Even without a legal ram in the bunch, they were entertaining to watch. The chopper was hovering around those sheep, causing them to tear off in all directions.

Nothing panics a wild animal so horribly as a helicopter. Harassment of that sort in that type of terrane is known to result in broken legs of the game being pursued. I figured the chopper was owned or chartered by a big oil exploration company. I was seriously irked.

The pilot made pass after pass close to the sheep, which led me to expect them to touch down and let someone get out to shoot one. After well over a half hour of harassing the animals the aircraft turned toward our camp. I decided to stay out of sight in my sleeping tent to see what the chopper people would do if they thought the camp was not occupied.

Sure enough, the Bell Jet Ranger landed near our camp and, with engine running, disgorged two men who walked directly to the cook tent, untied the flap, and went inside. With my rifle in hand I followed them inside and in an unfriendly tone asked what they thought they were doing in my tent.

At the sound of my voice they spun around and stepped toward me offering to shake hands. I told them to stay right there and identify themselves. The older man said he was Senator Ernest Gruening. I recognized him as he said his name and replied, "You mean former Senator, don't you?" Gruening had been defeated in 1968 by Mike Gravel, but still had a strong presence on the Alaska political stage.

He stammered a bit, but put forth that they were surveying the Skolai Pass area, taking photos and helping determine if that area should be afforded special protection, perhaps even designation as a new National Park area.

My comments and demeanor were correctly perceived as hostile and Gruening asked for permission to depart. I asked what his idea was in entering our tent without so much as a shout to see if anyone was inside, - possibly naked, or otherwise compromised. The younger man, whose name I cannot recall was becoming agitated, so I told him that they were trespassing and I did not appreciate it.

Ernest Gruening was territorial governor here from 1939 to 1953 and U.S. senator from Alaska 1958 to 1968.

I reminded Senator Gruening that it was not considered good manners to enter another person's tent in their absence, or anytime short of an emergency, without their permission. The conversation was strained and brief after this exchange. I was a bit wound up, I guess.

Both men stuttered out profuse apologies and asked my permission to just leave. I wish I had taken pictures of them or us together, but the thought never crossed my mind at the time. I escorted them to the still running helicopter and noticed another man in the back seat. They were soon up and away.

I made myself a cup of hot chocolate.

The rest of our time in Skolai Pass that season was pretty routine, if hunting can ever be so. Our guests all took rams that put smiles on their faces and no one sustained injuries other than a couple of blisters and sore muscles. I kept mulling over the possibility of hunting being forbidden in this great area in the near future.

In late September, I stopped by the Anchorage Book Cache which was downtown and close to Pennys to find some reading material for my fall travels. I glanced at a new Charles M. Russell book, which had photos of many of his wonderful oil paintings of Montana in the late 1800s up through the 1930s. He had long been my favorite western artist.

As I was paying for my purchases I suggested to the clerk that someone should request of Fred Machetanz that he produce a collection of his Alaskan oils in a book form, thereby making it possible for aficionados to have a nice set of his works.

The clerk suggested that I ask him, myself. I replied, "Sure, like I walk in the same circles, so maybe I'll just pop over to New York or where ever he lives and ask him.

She said suggested that I just turn around and ask him, right then. Fred Machetanz was behind me in the check out line, smiling. Then, I recognized him - he was the man in the back seat of the chopper in Skolai Pass!

Fred said, "Hey, I know you. You're the guy with the rifle, protecting your tent in Skolai Pass last month."

Fred and I shook hands and went outside to visit. Fred told me that he had cautioned Senator Gruening not to enter the tent and refused to join him.

Learning that I lived in Kotzebue, Fred suggested that I send him some photo slides of pack ice, for which he would pay $5 each and possibly use them in his painting. I told him that I would be honored to send him slides and if they were of use to him, that was reward enough for me. I spent that night at his home on High Ridge, near Palmer, enjoyed one of his famous margaritas and headed off to Valdez the following morning.

Over the years I sent Fred Machetanz dozens of slides from the Arctic and he mailed me many checks, none of which I ever cashed. I was pleased to send him and Sara frozen caribou meat, sheefish and occasionally whale meat and muktuk, as they enjoyed those and other wild foods as much as I do.

In 1978, I took some bush meat to Fred and he ushered me downstairs, where he gave me an original oil painting of eskimos in an umiak, with the harpooner about to deliver the coup de grace to an already struck bowhead whale, with a shoulder gun. It is 27 X 34 inches in size, beautifully framed and hangs in my office, worth far more than the uncashed checks which I still have. I was humbled by his generosity and even more by his friendship.

Their home at High Ridge was very comfortable.

I was often a guest of Fred and his lovely wife, Sara.

Fred's beloved wife, Sara, passed away in September, 2001 and he followed her in death in October, 2002. They were married for 54 years. They were two of the most wonderful Alaskans I have been privileged to know.

Hunting and guiding have brought me many wonderful memories. My association with the Machetanz' was one of the finest.

337 Pound Halibut

My earliest memories of fishing were of sitting on a bank of the Rio Grande next to my Dad, hoping for a catfish to nibble and later, with Grandpa in many places along the coast of South East Texas, where most anything might become attached to the line. I liked the salt water fishing better. One time we caught a strange looking fish called a Gaspergoo. The variety and mystery of ocean fishing attracted me and fed my imagination.

Alaskans are so richly blessed with fishing opportunities. During my first summer I explored and exploited the waters of Resurrection Bay, catching silver salmon off the dock, before I began using a rented 12 foot riveted aluminum boat with a 15 hp engine to improve my chances. On two occasions, silver salmon actually jumped right into my little boat! It seems like I always came home with a cooler full of fillets.

How it is that some "good" fishermen seem to consistently catch bigger fish than we amateurs has always stumped me. Random dumb luck would seem to be the biggest factor, but I have so often seen the experienced experts consistently haul out the biggest and most fish, that I often find myself mulling over the issue. In my own case, catching a big fish is due primarily, no, exclusively to random, dumb luck. I do my best on "blind pig" days.

Prior to that memorable day in mid July, 1990, the biggest fish that had affixed itself to my string was a halibut that weighed about 150 pounds. I was content with that, thanking my lucky stars, without having any dreams of besting that personal record.

My friend, Devoe Friend (yes, that was his real name,- Friend), had offered to take six of us locals to Whale Pass for a day of bottom fishing. The weather and sea conditions were favorable and I was delighted to accept the kind offer. DeVoe was one of those rare phenomenally blessed fishermen who always seemed to catch the most and biggest fish.

The sun came out and the wind went slack and as so often comes with such circumstances, the fishing was slack, too. We were catching a few medium sized Pacific Cod and some very small halibut, - chickens - which we were releasing. Having tried several spots, Devoe anchored the skiff in about 40 feet of water midway in Whale Pass on the north side. It was one of those rare, sunny warm days and I began to feel sleepy. I thought the chances of catching a keeper halibut in that shallow area were not so great, but the chances of a nice nap were very good and I was resolved to attempt a siesta. I had filleted a cod of about 20 inches in length, gave the fillets to others to use as bait and decided to use the carcass, for my bait, hooking it through the upper lip and dropping it over the side of the boat. It seductively waved in the gentle current.

I was seduced in the direction of a nap. I ate a sandwich, generously slathered with mayonnaise, tied my rod to the rail and settled back on the gunnel to doze. I was soon asleep, only to be disturbed by a very determined force on my fishing rod. I imagined that a submerged drift log had engaged my line and was being pushed by the current, but I saw nothing.

Devoe noticed my bent rod and said he thought I had a rock. I was not sure, but then the reel began to click as the big fish attempted to swim away. It was not a rock and not a log, this thing was alive!

Six of the seven rods on board had double hooked, baited lines in the water, so Devoe told everyone to bring their lines in to avoid entangling with whatever I had on mine. As this was not the first halibut I had ever caught, I was pretty sure from the feel of its runs that indeed, it was a big flatfish. The braided 80 pound test line was stained and old in appearance which was usually the case with Devoe's gear. I began to wonder - expect is a better description of my emotion - if before the fish could be brought up for a look, let alone be harpooned, it might separate the line. I treated the line and fish as carefully as possible, expecting it to go slack and empty at any moment.

It took only about 35 minutes to bring the fish up almost within harpoon range, but when it sensed the boat, it waved it's tail and headed west toward the deeper water at the mouth of the pass. It was a monster halibut! The reel

Pat, Devoe and Jake. Fish - 84 inches long, 337 pounds.

screamed as line stripped off, Devoe dipped his coffee cup in the water to pour on my reel to cool it. By reflex I placed my thumb on the spool and when I applied pressure to add to the drag, my fingerprints were burned off before I could correct my mistake.

This was a big, powerful fish.

I cranked the monster back nearly to within range for a harpoon thrust, but it was too "green" and repeated its escape drill. Neither time did the fish break the surface.

The third time I brought the fish to the boat, everyone was peering over the side, which caused quite a list on the twenty foot skiff, but also lowered the gunnel, facilitating Devoe's thrust. He drove the harpoon through the top gill plate and out the opposite side - a perfect strike! The fish was momentarily stunned, but after about 3 seconds it exploded and ran about twenty feet until checked by the harpoon line which was secured to the rail.

What a fish!

Devoe told us all that was the biggest fish he had ever seen, as he let the leviathan battle the harpoon line, still attached to my fishing line, as well. One of the guests, Frank, had a .44 magnum pistol and offered to shoot the halibut. I was accustomed to just breaking a gill or cutting the throat, but in this case the pistol seemed a good idea. As the fish began to slack off in it's struggles to escape, I pulled it in alongside the skiff and Frank's pistol shot to the head immediately rolled the brute.

Poleaxed and belly up, it was!

My sister, Pat, got most of this, including the pistol shot on video film.

It was all Devoe, Frank and I could do, to pull that mega fish into the skiff. Once boated, a line around the tail was passed through the gills and drawn tight, restraining the fish in a flexed position, to prevent the critter from thrashing, and possibly causing serious injury to someone in the boat.

We had been engaged in landing that one fish for over an hour, so after stowing all the gear it was time to head for town.

According to the table in the tide book, it weighed 337 pounds and was exactly 84 inches,- 7 feet in length. I retrieved the otoliths (ear bones) for eventual conversion to earrings for Teresa.

A reporter from the Kodiak Daily Mirror came by for photographs and the story. When asked what it weighed, I told him that I estimated it at somewhat less than 900 pounds.

I've always been a stickler for accuracy in fish tales.

Pacific halibut (Hippoglossus stenolepis) are the largest of the world's several types of flatfish. The largest sport caught halibut weighed 459 pounds and was over 8 feet in length.

But mine was big enough for me.

Alan's Big Kings

I met my good friend Alan, a maker of fine wines and brandy, when he came up to hunt Moose and Caribou with me in the Arctic. Our friendship went way beyond casual and a couple years later, we hunted together at his favorite Mule deer spot in Idaho and we kept in close touch.

Unfortunately, Alan developed an aggressive form of Lymphoma and eventually he wound up in an isolation tent in a hospital in Seattle. Essentially, the treatment called for killing off his bone marrow and I don't know what all else. But he lived in the sterile tent, protected from viruses and bacteria until his immune system could build up sufficiently to allow him to circulate once again with humans and the rest of the world.

Alan was a very strong man, both physically and mentally. His recovery was remarkably rapid. I received several hand written letters from him, some of which he told me took a week for him to write. He steadily regained his strength and was able to enjoy his hunting and fishing pursuits as before. It looked like he had licked the cancer, but after about three years, it came back. The prognosis was guarded and the outlook was grim.

Alan had mentioned to me that he always wanted to catch a fifty pound Chinook. I told him that fish of that size are not commonly caught in the Kodiak area, and I had never personally landed one that large, but I encouraged him to come, and we would give it our best shot.

When he arrived the weather turned beautiful. My sister, Pat, accompanied Alan and I for a long day trip down the Eastern shores of Kodiak. We hit all the known "hot spots" but had not so much as seen a salmon, not even a Pink! I went further that day than I had gone before in looking for salmon and had the least to show for the effort.

As we headed home that evening I slowed down and trolled by a wash rock off Cape Gravel, thinking that we might at least pick up a nice Lingcod. Alan's pole bent nearly double and he hollered that it felt like he had something large on the end of his line. Pat brought her line in to avoid a tangle. Whatever it was acted like a King, but was soon off. Probably it had been hooked by the skin of it's lip, but it had been a big one, at any rate.

Circling the boat to make another pass, I put out both down riggers and at nearly the same spot, Alan again hooked into a large fish. Pat got her gear out of the water and I brought up both down rigger balls.

This was a huge King Salmon for sure and Alan told us that he didn't care how much it weighed, it was the biggest he had ever felt on a line. I told him to pay attention and land the fish.

That Chinook came within sight of the boat three times and each time it dove hard beneath us. I had both my outboards raised or it would have no doubt snagged and broken off.

On the forth time to the boat, I got the fish in the landing net. I had landed a 49 pound King once a few years earlier, but this fish was deeper and longer and clearly outweighed my best. It was bound to tip the scales at over fifty pounds.

The sun was dropping toward the horizon, but I lowered one outboard and rigged up again. Alan immediately hooked up with another large fish. This one was more active than the first and nearly as large, but after five approaches to the boat, I got a net over it and we had it on the deck. My word, those two soakers, the two biggest salmon that had been boated on the LADY SASQUATCH were taken within minutes of each other. The limit is two King Salmon per day and Alan said he was done, but he wanted us to keep fishing.

Late or not, we made another pass at the wash rock and Pat hooked up with a dandy that weighed 35 pounds, then another that made 33 pounds.

By then we were about twenty miles from town and a dark, moonless night was developing. There had been a fair amount of flotsam, including some large logs liberated by the big monthly tides, so we would have to proceed slowly in the dark. It was time to head for home.

Alan and his 55 pound White King.

Alan with his Kings. The kids got out of bed to see them.

In my basement I have a very accurate counter balance scale. Alan's first Chinook weighed 55 pounds, 5 ounces and his second tipped the scale at 52 pounds 6 ounces. To top it all off, they were both white Kings!

Things just don't get much better than that! And it couldn't have happened to a better person. As of this writing in 2013, I have yet to claim a fifty pound Chinook.

Skatin' for Halibut

Sitting at anchor or drifting on the tide with a heavy sinker and bait for halibut has never been my favorite form of fishing. Yes, we've had some really good days, but we've had slow ones, too. When out with the boat I'd rather be more actively pursuing fish by trolling for salmon or jigging for rockfish and lingcod. Nevertheless, we used hook and lines for halibut for years. As my daughters have grown up, they have always been able to truthfully say that they caught fish larger than they were. Each has landed halibut of 150 pounds or more.

My wife yearned to catch a big one and when she finally did, in 1998 we were anchored on a sea mount about twenty miles offshore. We'd been using jigs and pulling up Black Rockfish of up to ten pounds each, when Teresa said that she had something much bigger on her line. It took her forty minutes to bring it up close enough to see and it was truly a monster flatfish. It made a run and disappeared into the depths, luckily the hook was firmly embedded in its jaw bone. I told her to bring it up to just below the surface, being careful to not have the fish actually break the surface, as that tends ot set them off on another run. When she got it up again, I thrust the harpoon into the gill plates and the toggle head penetrated completely through to the opposite side. After I stuck another iron into the big fish, I cut its throat to bleed it well. When it ceased thrashing I was able to get it up over the rail and into the boat. That was the largest fish that our daughters, then 3 and 4 years old had ever seen. They were proud of Mom.

As always, as soon as I had the fish in the boat, I bound the tail to the head, keeping the fish in an arched position and thereby immobilizing it.

A fish of that size and power can do serious damage to people and equipment if allowed to flop about on the deck. Broken legs have been reported by halibut fishermen numerous times.

A dense fog bank was moving in from the east, but Teresa wanted to keep fishing. She was sure that another, even bigger halibut awaited her bait, just below us. It seemed that she, herself, was hooked.

Her premonition was correct and no sooner had her sinker hit bottom than her reel was whining as the second big fish made it's first run.

My observation and prediction of the heavy fog was correct also. Soon our visible world had shrunken to about twenty feet from the sides of the boat. We were going to have a slow trip home.

This fish took a bit more time to bring up, but I got an iron in it at the first opportunity. That fish exploded, but the harpoon line, tied to an inside rail, checked it's run and abruptly brought it up short after only a short struggle... So, we soon had that one on the deck alongside the first.

We pulled anchor and headed west, toward Kodiak.

As one might expect, my radar quit that day, but the compass was fine, and that was enough to get us home.

Until 2010, we fished for personal use halibut using rods and reels as described. But Halibut fishing was pretty slow in 2010. I had heard nothing but tales of woe from Kodiak sport fishing operators and commercial fishermen told me that the fish they were turning in were averaging less than 15 pounds each - and that just ain't good.

My sister and I had commercially fished for halibut in the 1990s from my 24 foot aluminum boat, the *F/V SASQUATCH* until the Feds changed the regulations. Individual Fishing Quotas were awarded to some fishermen and were available for sale to people like us, but I viewed that as privatization of a public resource and would have no part of it. So the only commercial halibut fishing I had done since enactment of the IFQs (Individual Fishing Quotas) was as a deck hand on bigger boats of those blessed with halibut quota.

The Feds had established a Subsistence Halibut fishery a few years before, and as residents of Kodiak, my family qualified for a permit. So we each got a "SHARC" card. That card allowed each of us to use a long line with up to 30 hooks for personal use in halibut fishing. I still had our old long line gear, so I figured that was the way to go. I cut lengths with 30 hooks and we were ready to long line again.

At first we just caught big brittle starfish, or "slops" in local lingo. Fish move around and we kept trying different spots, based on previous experience and the sonar picture of the bottom. On the third day of "soaking" for four hours, we came back to our set and had a 50 pounder - near perfect size.

Salmon fishing was abysmally slow in 2010 also. Our girls no longer cared much about fishing, but they still liked catching. One day in mid July, after making one halibut long line set, Teresa and I went to a reef system a few miles offshore where we trolled through a huge biomass of bait fish. I estimated it at about 30 tons. With one down rigger at 60 feet and the other at 90 feet, we didn't get a hit. Teresa turned the boat as I switched lures, putting two black spoons on. On our

Another good day after fishing with poles.

next pass through the bait we each had a nice King Salmon. We were kept busy for the next forty minutes, until we had our limits - 2 Kings and 5 Silver Salmon, each. On the way back to port we found another 50 pound halibut on the long line.

So the next day, I suggested that the girls go catching with us. They agreed in anticipation of lots of great action.

We put out the long line in the same, protected spot as the day before, using salmon heads, split down the middle as bait on all but two hooks.

However when we reached the previous day's hot spot, I couldn't find any bait balls nor sign of bird activity, and we got no hits in four hours of trolling, plus the water had turned uncomfortably choppy.

On the way home we pulled the long line (also called a skate) and there, tangled in five hooks and one anchor was a barn door halibut. For the past several years, I had normally released the really big fish like that, as they are all females and important for spawning. Too many have been taken in recent years, probably contributing to the decrease in size of the average commercial catch. This fish was so entangled that I had to kill it. At home we measured it at 6 feet, 6 inches in length. The tide books give a pretty accurate estimated weight based on length and this fish would have been 254.7 pounds live weight, 191.5 pounds dressed.

After tying the tail we began pulling up the skate. The next fish was much bigger. It was pretty tired from fighting the long line, which enabled us to get an accurate length measurement. It was 8 feet, 3 inches long, giving it a live weight of about 550 pounds and would have dressed out at about 390 pounds. The big hen was tired but alive, so I cut the ganion and set her free. Maybe we'll catch some of her offspring in the future.

A third monster fish was on that line, but it escaped before we could measure it.

Our girls were reluctant to release the biggest fish we had ever caught, but I believe all huge halibut in excess of one hundred pounds live weight - unless damaged by the gear or handling, should be restricted from taking by anyone. They are much too important as brood stock.

With the dock price at $5.50 per pound and higher, and top prices paid for the really big hens, that largest fish would have brought over $2,700 to a commercial fisherman.

No one observed us fishing in our "secret hole", which is not far from Kodiak and our lips have remained sealed regarding the exact location. I plan to fish there in the future.

At home, getting the one we had out of the boat was a chore. I attached a line to the tail and used our second pickup to pull it out, over the rail and into a cart. In the carport I have a block and tackle for handling gill nets and other gear, so we raised the big flatfish for a picture and for ease of butchering.

The meat of such a huge fish is no less delicious than that of smaller ones, to my taste. We had more than enough for our own needs and plenty to share with friends and relatives. We did not put out the skate again that season.

The packaged and frozen flesh of that large fish was distributed to people from Kodiak, Anchorage, Fairbanks and Kotzebue.

Bess, Jake, Kate and Teresa with our biggest fish of 2010.

This Halibut measured
8 feet, 3 inches - a 550 pounder.

A thirty hook skate ready to set.

Kobuk Jade

In the early 1970s I met Bill Munz - entrepreneur extraordinaire. Bill had been in Alaska for many decades and did not ever waste any of his time. He had established and operated Munz Northern Airlines, serving as mechanic, pilot and business manager. The term greasy handed CEO would apply.

Bill's wealth of experience and stories of the area were of great interest to me. He wintered in Chloride, Arizona, where he had some mining claims, but returned to NW Alaska every summer. I met him one evening after he landed his Cessna 170 on the dirt strip in Kotzebue and had a flat tire. It turned out that his inner tube was ruined. I had several spares, so I gave him one. We went to my house for dinner and he stayed the night. When he passed through Kotzebue in the future he usually spent the night at our house. His inventory of great stories was wonderful to hear.

Bill always made good money and he kept investing it in what he knew to be sure deals. He owned several gold dredges on Seward Peninsula - all of which he had acquired at minimal cost after the gold business in remote Alaska had taken a nose dive during World War II. Bill also sold his stuff at very reasonable prices.

Mr. Munz loved gold and carried a small suitcase with some gold bars he had smelted at one of his holdings on Seward Peninsula. In the grip was also some hard rock gold mixed with quartz from Arizona and a few Kruger Rands, Austrian Ducats and other precious coins. He kept a small revolver in the suitcase - ready for immediate access, as well.

One old gold prospect up the Kobuk River, on Cosmos Creek, near the Dall Creek airport had caught his attention.

In the summer of 1898, false reports of a gold strike on the Kobuk suckered a couple thousand hopeful get rich quickers to that area of the Arctic. It never produced much gold or held promise of riches. Most of the boomers departed for better diggings in the Koyukuk and Nome fields.

In 1865 U.S. Navy Lt. George M. Stoney reported finding jade on the Shungnak River. (Shungnak is an anglicized approximation of the Inuit term for jade.)

In 1906 a German gold prospector reportedly sent jade from the area home to have a necklace made. But no one paid much attention to the jade for decades.

In 1944 a U.S. Bureau of Mines party, searching for asbestos for the war effort, rediscovered the jade, along with the asbestos and shipped five tons of jade out.

Huge boulders of green nephrite jade could be seen in creeks and lying on the hillsides in the upper Kobuk River country. In 1952, Kotzebue entrepreneur Archie Ferguson flew in a saw to cut jade boulders on site and got some out, but it was not enough of a money maker for him, so the country and its jade went lonesome.

In the 1960s, flumes, built in the century before by the gold miners to wash their dirt and gravel, were still in place. Bill Munz knew that he could get water flowing down the flumes to run large diamond saws to cut the big boulders. So he bought the claims.

On one of his overnights in Kotzebue, he asked me if I had time to work with him on jade that summer.

His plan was for me to take the super cub to Dahl Creek, then fly him at slow speed and low level down the narrow canyons, so he could give his full attention to spotting boulders. Then we would get his wannagin (a portable living shack) and use his D9 caterpillar to wrestle the boulders onto spruce sleds (called "go devils") for which we cut spruce trees on the spot and put together. Using the big caterpillar we would drag the boulders to either the work area which had the hydraulically powered saws or directly to a bank of the Kobuk, from which they could be pushed off directly onto barges headed back to the coast.

Returning to Kotzebue after delivering supplies up river, the barges were normally empty, so Bill had been cut a very inexpensive rate for moving the jade. It was just extra gravy for the barge company.

It sounded like fun to me … and potential profit. I was to get a share of the jade that made it to Kotzebue, my share depending on how much time and effort I put into the operation. Bill was a fair man. I agreed to his proposition.

Black bears and mosquitoes are thick in that area during June and July. I soon discovered that Deep Woods Off worked best on the bugs and served as a very pleasant cologne and deodorant as well.

No permits were necessary back then to cut timber or drag the go devils across virgin tundra to reach the banks of the river for delivery of the boulders. One could never do that without severe governmental repercussions nowadays.

Bill Munz was a good steward of the wilderness, though. He always avoided dragging repeated go devil loads over the same trail. To do so would have caused deep scars and damage to the tundra. After a year, the single use trails we made were barely noticeable.

Bill was a pleasure to be around. He spared little time for anything but work, but did spin some interesting tales of his adventurous life in rural Alaska - usually as he ate his spartan dinner. Each evening he would swallow two beers, not more and not less.

His work area was always fastidiously clean and organized. Not a nut or bolt was out of place. He often mentioned that he didn't know how disorganized people made it. If things were in their proper place, work was fast and efficient. It was a principle he lived by.

Every machine was always wiped clean. One could have stayed healthy eating off his floors.

Bill offered to sell his jade claims and equipment to me about 1977 or so. The price was much lower than I would have expected, but thinking it over, I would have to hire a mechanic to keep the Cat running, along with the other machinery at the cutting site. That was a negatory for me, plus I had so many interesting things to do already, I thanked him and told him I'd stay on with him as long as he wished, but did not want to run the operation.

Bill sold his claims and equipment to Ivan Stewart of Stewart's Photo in Anchorage.

I had built a 24 foot by 32 foot frame and plywood store for my wife Mae to run in 1974. We called it Arctic Rivers Trading Company.

Part of my share of the 1975 summer jade mining was a large stream polished slick boulder that we estimated to weigh about 16 tons. It had some opalescent areas showing on the exterior and had the beautiful deep green of what we called Kobuk Green Number One. I had the beautiful thing placed right in front of the store.

We had no worries about anybody chipping chunks off to steal. Jade is extremely hard, tough and heavy. That big green rock was a tourist attraction, and impervious to mischief or theft, for sure.

Not a week after the big fork lift placed the boulder, Mae said that an older gentleman from one of the Wien Air Alaska tourist groups had asked her how much I would sell it for. He intended to return to her store in the morning before heading back south.

Surprised at the prospect of selling the rock so soon, without too much contemplation I told her the price was $40,000. I was scheduled to fly a big game survey the next day and thought little more about the situation.

In November, I got a call from the fellow from St. Louis. He said the price for the jade piece was high and it would cost him a fortune to get it to Missouri. I told him that the price was probably too low, but it would cost him nothing to move it.

He asked if I intended to pay the freight bill to get it to his home.

"Transportation costs are not included in the sale price", I said, but He could leave it right where it was and I would not charge him a dime for the space rental.

Our conversation went on for awhile. He said he enjoyed visiting with me and asked if anyone else had bid on the rock. I told him that so far, he was the only one.

In January of 1976 he called again. He asked if a Cashier's Check would be ok with me for the boulder. I said it would be fine. He arranged to send his "man" up in May with the check and to arrange for shipment. Then he said he would send $1,000 as earnest money to seal the deal.

Wow! I was flabbergasted. I had expected that rock to sit where it was for many years, possibly forever. I immediately got out my graph paper and began figuring on a 24 foot by 60 foot addition to Mae's store. The next week I ordered the materials and scheduled them to be sent up on the first summer barge.

All along I assumed that the jade would go south on the barge that brought my building materials up, but the old fellow's "man" arrived well before the barge. When he handed me the bank draft he said the biggest fork lift available in town was coming from the lighterage company and his chartered Hercules freight plane was due the next morning.

Then I realized that I really had priced the boulder much too low. The cost of the charter to St. Louis was probably well over $50,000! Oh well, Mae would have her store tripled in size and I could get more jade that same summer.

It seemed to me that the old gentleman wanted to have some sort of grave site monument made of the jade, but I never did find out what became of that special stone.

The other pieces of jade that I got as shares were not so big as that one, but they were still pretty weighty. For Mae's store, we shipped some to Taipei, Taiwan for making into simple jewelry or carvings and a few we shipped to Eder-Oberstein, Germany. For all but the most intricate carvings, we used the Taiwan companies, as they charged a much lower price.

Bill, using his slow moving diamond edged drag saws, with a continuous oil drip, could slab off a table top from a boulder like the one below in about a week. We left them all with free form edges. They were very attractive and sold well.

The smaller boulders were either sold whole, especially the stream polished slicks that had a nice rind, or were slabbed off into beef steak sized pieces for use at hot pot holders, or put to whatever other use one might imagine.

Kobuk Valley Jade Company had saws and other gear to cut and prepare jade in Kotzebue until the owner shipped a lifetime supply of boulders to Anchorage, sold his shop in Kotzebue and set up at Alyeska, a ski area near Anchorage.

Probably the best jade claims in the area belonged to Gene Joiner. He had crashed is Piper Super Cruiser one winter and froze off some fingers and toes and had become a bitter old man, but he sold his claims, reportedly for $5 million dollars to the U.S. government, which then turned them over to the regional native corporation.

With brand new equipment, saws, etc. the corporation turned out some really nice jade tiles and other pieces for a few years, but then the business folded and has not been resumed.

One of the three Jade boulders I still have in Kotebue.

Word was that Logan Mountain in the Cassiar District of British Columbia came on line with their green nephrite jade which, since they were on the road system, was much less expensive to get to markets.

So that's how I got involved with a mining operation. Mining was my Dad's first interest, but way down the list for me. However, given the opportunity, I would jump right back into an endeavor like the one Bill Munz invited me to participate in. I think most of those opportunities are gone forever, unfortunately.

I still have three large jade boulders sitting in my yard in Kotzebue. One has been slabbed for a table top, showing the quality of the rock and its rind. The other two are uncut, just as nature produced them. And, of course, those boulders are for sale.

Frau Eder and Me

In 1989 I had booked a delightful couple from Austria, Edmund and Johanna Eder. As it was with most of my new European guests, they were referred to me by previous hunters from within their circle of acquaintances. They were totally unpretentious and very friendly.

During our last August booking period that year, the Eders were our only guest hunters at Trail Creek.

With neither of them having previously flown in small aircraft, the trip from Kotzebue to the lodge was an adventure for each of them, one at a time in my cub. Edmund was very solemn about the trip, smiling a lot and taking it all in. His wife was obviously a bit ill at ease, but not to the point of being uncomfortable. I remembered to make no tight turns as we looked at animals and I pointed out geographic features such as "pingos" and frost polygons, during the hour and a half flight.

Moose were still holding tight in the willow patches and we had seen only a few in the valley near the lodge, so I decided to take Edmund back to Kotzebue, then use the float plane to check out one of my other favorite moose areas.

On our first night using the tent, Edmund, a pharmacist by trade, gave me a bit of an education on wild mushrooms. As I returned to the campsite after glassing for Moose, he was sitting next to the small fire, roasting some small, suspicious, psychedelically colored mushrooms that are commonly found that time of year, sprouting from goose poop. I cautioned him that they might have a adverse, even deadly effect on those who consumed their flesh, but he said the same type grew in the mountains of Austria and he was sure they were safe. But I did not partake of that particular delicacy. As we were about to nod off for the night, Edmund told me that one could eat any mushroom he found, but some could only be eaten once.

That was a discomforting thought.

The next morning, Edmund took a fine bull moose and we spent the next night at my shack in Kotzebue, dining on filet mignon of Moose and boxed red wine.

Hansi, as Edmund called Johanna, his Frau, had been enjoying her stay at the lodge with Teresa and my sister, Pat. She was impressed with the giant Boletus mushrooms and others that were abundant that year, but they had only seen cow and calf Moose.

Another trip with the float plane was clearly called for. Edmund assured Hansi that she would enjoy the experience very much and told her of the thirty or more bulls we had seen from the air during the hour before landing. Her enthusiasm was apparent and the next day, we bid goodbye to the camp and headed for town.

As I approached Kotzebue I asked for the Terminal Forecast, the Area Forecast and the Outlook. It sounded like we could expect to enjoy a solid three days of light winds and dry conditions, followed by a significant blow, caused by the remains of an old typhoon system in the South Pacific that was tracking our way. Most Moose trips of this nature took only one or two nights in a tent, so I plunged ahead with our plans.

Departing Kotzebue about three hours before dark, we flew directly to the area just vacated by Edmund and I. Things change rapidly in the Arctic as summer yields to autumn and Fau Eder and I found many more Moose ambling about that evening than her husband and I had encountered just three days earlier.

We found capital bulls in nearly every part of a foothills area with lots of lakes adequate for a super cub operation scattered about conveniently. I elected to stay well away from the area of the recent kill, as both Black and Grizzly bears are abundant in that country and some would have no doubt located the gut pile of Edmund's bull and would be nearby, still.

I put the camp in a particularly nice location on a lake situated on the edge of a large escarpment, with a grand view of the surrounding hillsides and well sheltered by large black spruce trees. As we circled to land, I saw four world class bulls within less than a mile and only slightly uphill from the lake.

A small fire was warranted and we dined on Moose backstrap, stick bread, apple pie heated in aluminum foil and, of course, red wine. A pair of loons serenaded us with their crazy calls and we heard a wolf howl in the distance. It was as if scripted by a screen writer, which, I guess it was, as God had directed it all. Within a hour of sundown, we were both tucked in and soon asleep.

Edmund and his bull.

As the sun began to hint of it's imminent appearance, I had the small fire making the coffee water boil and Frau Eder was preparing to meet the day in good spirits. There was no chill that morning, as a heavy overcast had moved in to hold the previous day's heat.

We were soon off to the hills south of the lake in hope and expectation of seeing one of the huge bulls. In less than an hour we located two great Moose, but neither was as good as the best I recalled from the evening before, which had solid palms and lots of points on each side. We had time to search. I was determined to find the best bull possible for this lady hunter and was confident that we would do so. We were standing at the edge of a copse of spruce trees and remained there, glassing carefully until well past mid day. I laid down on the soft, dry moss and dozed off while Frau Eder kept vigilantly searching with her binoculars for the great bull.

As usual, I had tossed a roll of sausage, some bisquits, two pieces of fruit and some candy bars into my pack. I figured we should hang right there until nearly dark, so the snacks were consumed with gusto in that fresh wild country air.

As I was contemplating a return to the campsite, the best bull showed his rack at the far edge of the willow patch for a few brief moments, then he merged back into the brush. I had enough of a look at him to be certain it was the one we wanted. We headed back to the camp, planning to come back the next morning.

A breeze of about fifteen miles per hour had developed out of the southeast quarter, but our tent was in the lee of the great spruce trees and therefore not adversely affected.

We spent that night as the one before, but did not hear the wolves.

The wind picked up in intensity that night, causing the tent to flap and pop at times. This was Frau Eder's first time in such a shelter and she slept little, but did not complain even once.

Coffee took a little more time to make in the wind of the morning, but along with store bought bear claw pastries, it was very much appreciated before we struck off to our Moose stand.

As we cautiously approached the spot we had been using, I saw all three big bulls standing, looking at each other less than eighty yards away. I turned my head to look at Frau Eder, standing ready just behind and to my left. I gave her the thumbs up signal to load quietly. After she silently slid a round home, I smiled and gave a shallow nod - "okay". She raised her rifle, took careful aim and hit the bull in the withers. The Moose spun around and ran toward us, quartering to our right. I told the lady to shoot again and she did, immediately. I heard the dull smack of the 30:06 slug burying itself into the shoulder of the Moose as it headed for parts beyond this place. Then the huge animal stopped, looked back at it's companions, raising its nose in the air, as it's hind legs folded. It fell over backward, - it had bled out internally and was stone dead.

Frau Eder and her superb Moose.

Frau Eder was not able to conceal her excitement, nor was I. This was an exceptionally fine example of Alces gigas, the giant Alaskan Moose. The two companion bulls slowly wandered off into heavy cover.

As we took pictures, I noticed that the wind had picked up and was gusting enough to make me want to check the plane. I cut the head off, then butchered the Moose as I usually do, leaving the hide on the four quarters to shield the meat from rain and discourage bird damage. Then I loaded the backstraps on my pack board. I hand carried the two huge tenderloins in a small net sack and we headed back to our camp.

The wind was right on the tail of the cub and had caused it to cockeye a bit, so I tightened up the securing lines and placed gust locks on the flaps, ailerons and rudder. It seemed that the old typhoon had arrived earlier than forecast.

With my ax, I cut and arranged some willows to place the meat on, keeping it off the damp ground and allowing air to circulate beneath. More leafy willows were placed on top to reduce the transmission of smells and discourage birds.

The moose dropped only about a fifteen minute pack from the lake and it was slightly downhill, so the meat hauling was not too bad at all. Seven more loads and I had all the meat and the head back at the meat cache, which was a couple hundred yards down the lake shore from our campsite. It seemed like the wind was getting stronger by the minute and by late afternoon was well over fifty miles per hour, coming directly across the lake. As the ground level airstream came over the hills bordering the little lake, the turbulence fairly boiled, creating the severe gusts I had been feeling all afternoon.

Frau Eder was wanting to get back to town, but the cross wind component was too much for comfortable and safe take-off, which I carefully explained to her.

Then the rain hit us, falling in large drops and coming hard a'crosswise. I put off skinning out the Moose head for later. The tent needed more lines on it to withstand the gusts, but some 550 nylon parachute chord did the trick adequately.

There would be no fire during this storm, so we dined on canned corned beef, cheese, crackers, fruit and cookies. We shared the last of the red wine. Not bad fare, under the circumstances. Then Frau Eder produced a small flask of her home made pear brandy! I always carry a book or two, but reading was out of the question with all the racket and buffeting from the wind. I told a few stories and emphasized the great size and high quality of the fine bull she had taken. She agreed that it would overpower the collection of red deer and rheboks that already hung in their home.

As darkness approached I went again to check the float plane and found several small blackfish that had been blown out of the lake and were flopping piteously on the moss. Prior to that, I had not been aware of their presence in this region. I had heard that they were a popular food item in the Bethel area, but by the time we could make a fire, they had lost their appeal, so I never did taste one.

That old, supposedly dissipating typhoon kept at it for all the next day, so we were camp bound. On one of my trips to find a bush, behind which to make my daily deposit, I found the skeleton of a large bull moose that had been killed earlier that month by a big Grizzly, judging from the poop and other sign left at the kill site. It was not far from our camp site and much too close for comfort. The rack of the bear kill was of real trophy quality. I brought the head and antlers back near our tent, but did not explain to Frau Eder how I assumed the animal had met it's end. There was no point in elevating her anxiety. As it was, she just admired this second huge rack of the day. I hoped the big Grizz would not amble into our camp, or find our meat cache.

I always keep my .44 magnum pistol close when camping and sometimes had a round chambered in my rifle, just in case. I've so far never been bothered by a bear while in a tent, but it has happened to others, with terrible consequences.

On the evening of our third night in the tent, the wind seemed to get tired and slacked off noticeably. Frau Eder asked if we might go back to town that night, but the overcast made my decision to remain an easy one. I never cared much for night flying, but with no clear skies and no moonlight, it would have been extra risky. And, there was no emergency. I felt comfortable about making a fire, at last, and we wolfed down fresh Moose meat, a baked potato, stick bread, cheese and fresh fruit for dinner.

Frau Eder was holding up well throughout all of this, her first experience in a tent camp. Storms can cause people to do some strange, panicky things, especially when they are clearly out of their element, but she was a stalwart soul, for sure.

Before morning, the sky had cleared, the temperature had fallen to a comfortable +34 degrees and we were more than pleased to load the back straps, tenderloins, moose head, camp materials and Frau Eder and I for the trip straight back to town. I got her back to the shack, suggested she have a shower, and relax with some wine. Back at the float pond, I refueled the cub and returned for the bulk of the Moose meat.

As I approached the lake I flew over the gut pile and saw a large Grizzly dining on the remaining delicacies. Apparently it had just discovered the place and would likely have soon found the meat cache had I been delayed in retrieving it.

I felt lucky all around.

Best Moose, Ever

In June, 1974 I got a call from a doctor in Texas who wanted to send his son, Tom, up to hunt Caribou as a high school graduation gift. The young man needed to hunt in early August as his college classes would begin shortly after mid-month.

The booking was confirmed and the young fellow arrived about August 8. He was all eyes for everything. Kotzebue usually seems like a foreign country to most first timers from the "South 48" and this young man was typical in that regard. He stated that it looked like a giant Arctic slum.

He stayed at our home that evening in town. Weather was good for a shot to the cabin the next morning, so we loaded up and headed north.

Initially, I thought he was hollering for "EUROPE", then I thought he might be calling for "RALPH", but actually, Tom began to get air sick before we were out of sight of town and was having the most wretched trip of anyone I'd ever transported. He'd brought a barf bag and filled it, then was heaving into his cap. When he ran out of stomach contents, his dry heaving really sounded painful.

I forbade him from emptying either his bag or his hat out the window as the contents would be plastered and soon wind dried on the fuselage of the cub. Vomit is extremely adherent when wind dried to aircraft fabric. Even after efficient scrubbing, the residual smell would attract bears which might do serious damage to our sole means of transportation back to town.

So Tom tended his containers with the utmost care.

About two thirds of the way to the cabin I offered to land for awhile, but he said he just wanted to get to the cabin and not have to fly anymore. We had about a half hour left to fly. After 15 minutes, near the mouth of Trail Creek, I saw a moose (Alces alces gigas) that looked like it was carrying two sheets of plywood on it's head! I had to circle back for a closer look. Poor Tom just moaned at the turn, however gently I manipulated the plane. I told him how outstanding this critter was, to which he replied that if it was a holdover Irish Elk from the last ice age, he didn't care. He just wanted to land and go to bed! I made two passes to convince myself of my appraisal.

What a Moose! And it had a companion sporting nearly the same antler dimensions! Wow! I sure hoped they would continue on up toward the cabin.

By this time, I had been living in Alaska for over seven years and had never seen lightening or heard thunder. A couple of days into Tom's week booking some dark cumulus clouds came up the valley. We were posted on a high point about a mile from the cabin. Seeing the clouds, Tom told me that he had been struck by lightening once and sure didn't want to experience that again.

I confidently told him that I'd never seen lightening and not to worry. "Trust me", I said.

The wind picked up and blew those towering cumulus right toward us. And yes, I knew that Murphy was with me as soon as the first big bolt of lightening cracked near the runway. Tom was spooked and no doubt sure that I was either crazy or an outright liar! Big drops of rain soaked us as we made our way back to the cabin. I counted over 20 strikes accompanied by deafening thunder. I was concerned that the aircraft and/or cabin might be hit.

Topographical maps of the area show a peak named Thunder Mountain about 12 miles from us, and of course, Tom noticed that. Now I understood why it was so named.

Grizzly season didn't open until the first of September, however the bears came out in force right after the heavy rain. These were the first bears that Tom had ever seen, other than in Walt Disney movies. I told him not to worry as we had rifles and besides, Grizzlies never ate people, they would just bite and scratch their human catches.

Tom gave me a quizical look.

Just before turning in for the night we went outside to pee and a single bear appeared in the swamp adjacent to the cabin and followed the trail toward us. With rifle in hand I advanced toward the bear and yelled. The Grizzly stood up to see us better, then dropped on all fours and ran back in the direction from which it had come.

My cooking has never been what I would call really great, but it comes with a guarantee - that if those who consume it can keep it down, it will make a turd.

Mother nature began to summon Tom about 3:00 AM. I heard him scuffling around in the little cabin (I just had a 12 foot by 12 foot plywood cabin at that time) and asked him what was up. He told me he had to take a dump and was trying to find a can or something, as he didn't want to go outside, drop his drawers and be vulnerable to that bear.

After the lightening strikes I figured there was no use trying to talk Tom out of bear danger, so I accompanied him to the outhouse, standing guard with my rifle. Pooping in the cabin was not an option for anyone. Tom was fast with his job and the paperwork. No bear appeared.

Spring migration brings Caribou north for calving in an area about 35 miles north of my place, followed by "post calving aggregational movements of large herds throughout the Western Books Range. Some Caribou usually hang out in the high meadows around my camp, and we saw the occasional lone bull, but Tom never had a decent opportunity to take one, yet.

Overall, Tom was a good guest, caught a few fish and saw plenty of Dall sheep, in addition to bears, moose and a wolf.

When we returned to town the news was full of the story of a world famous photographer who had pitched his tent on a bear trail on the Alaskan Peninsula. This guy was in his tent when a large bear attacked, demolishing his tent and gear and eating all but his feet which were found securely laced into his leather boots. Tom heard all of this, but did not discuss it with me. My credibility with this young man was about a low as it could be. Of that, I was sure.

I kept thinking about that monstrous moose. On every flight to the cabin, rather than going directly, I would sashay around looking at the willow patches, cottonwood groves and side streams in hopes of finding him again. Several times I searched the main Kugururuk River, finding lots of moose, but not either of those two humongous bulls. I had no photograph of them, but their images were indelibly etched in my memory.

In late August I took two hunters up to the cabin, one at a time in the cub. On the second trip I found a bunch of moose about 12 miles downstream and amongst them were the two giant bulls! I told the hunter just how outstanding they were, but he told me that ALL moose looked huge to him.

Normally I did not fly much after getting guest hunters to the cabin, except to put in a tent camp. However, with those two moose headed our way, on a couple of evenings, just before dark I would load one guest in the back and take off to monitor the moose. They kept moving north, toward the cabin.

The two guest hunters were good company. They were awed by the wilderness, the variety and abundance of game and fish and their entire experience. Each shot a nice bull caribou. Next they wanted moose. I felt it likely that they would get opportunities to take those two giants.

By late August moose normally begin to shed the velvet from their antlers, making their headgear stand out like headlights. The big fellows were no exception to this and it made keeping track of them much easier. A few days passed and using a spotting scope from a nearby vantage point I located the two giants on Popple Creek, about 5 miles down stream from the cabin. I figured they were bound to come right on up and be more easily accessible.

The next morning we spotted some decent bulls in a willow patch just off the end of my main runway. I estimated their width at between 55 and 60 inches. They were good bulls, but not the giants!

Our guests had discussed an overnight in Anchorage to allow a trip to the Great Alaska Bush Company (a strip joint featuring total nudity). The more they talked about that visit, the more attractive an early departure, allowing them to spend two nights at the Bush Company became to them. The two bulls close to the end of the runway became just too much of a temptation. They wanted to shoot them and head south. I couldn't convince them to do otherwise.

As we walked down for those moose I half way hoped they would bugger out, escaping us which would soon force an opportunity at the giants, but that was not to be. Both hunters got a nice bull. They cheerfully helped pack the meat and antlers back to the cabin and that was that! They talked more about the Bush Company than their fine trophies.

The next day I took them each to Kotzebue with their moose antlers and saw them board the Alaska Airlines jet for Anchorage … and the girls.

When I got back to the house in Kotzebue, my wife and daughter came out to meet me and show me that the Bronco had some damage. The story was, my daughter, Sandy, had somehow driven the Bronco into the ocean, but she had the presence of mind to get help to drag it back ashore, then got the engine started and drove it home. Once safely in the yard, she was so excited that she missed the brake and hit the throttle instead, jamming the front of the Bronco into the wheel well of the pickup. Dandy deal!

I kept my temper, only to notice that our two story addition to the back of the house had collapsed in a big wind storm.

I'd helped a local fellow get set up as a contractor and had a formal contract with him to do the framing and outside plywood for the addition. Story was, he had been hiring some guys from the Air Force Dew Line site, but decided to use a couple of high school boys instead to save on what he was paying in wages. The day of the accident, winds had been gusting to 70 mph and the wannabe contractor was trying to put up a second story wall that was ten feet high and 36 feet in width assisted by a single high school teenager. The siding was already nailed in place, creating a huge sail, inviting the wind to do its worst.

His judgment was not good, to say the least. Anyway, a gust of wind blew the wall over, taking the contractor with it and breaking both of his legs.

One of the air force men came by and told me the details and that he heard the contractor was planning to sue me! Well, hell's sakes! I was pretty sure that I was not vulnerable to a lawsuit and was so disgusted with things in town, I told my wife, Mae, to just get packed, as we were going up to the cabin. It was just too crazy and stressful in town!

Our flight was pleasant, and as I was setting up to land, I saw the two great bulls about a mile down the creek, walking slowly up stream.

1974 was the first year that one could not take a moose until after 3:00 am of the day following flight, so we landed and had our supper, with lots of interruptions to check if the moose were visible off the end of the runway which bordered a clear area that they were likely to cross. By dark, we'd seen no sign of them, so we went to bed, but we slept little in our excited state.

Before daylight I was on the roof of the little cabin, seated in a folding chair, glassing down creek with a cup of coffee in hand. I'd decided to climb into the hills to the east for better viewing when, and if, the bulls appeared.

At first light they were walking fast right up the riverbed. I informed Mae, who quickly joined me on the roof. I began making cow calls, a low moaning noise that the bulls keyed in on immediately. They stopped, then turned directly up the main runway and were coming to the cabin. There was not time enough for us to intercept them on the runway, so we stayed right there, on the roof with maximum visibility. The moose hesitated in the nearest patch of willows, offering no clear shot, but I moaned again and they both walked right into our yard. The lead bull was the better of the two and we had agreed that only the larger one would be shot. I told Mae to fire and she hit the bull in the chest with her 130 grain .270 slug. Both bulls wheeled and turned to run. When I fired my .300 WinMag, hitting the bull just behind the shoulder, he stopped. He began to sway, then raised his head high and fell over backwards. We had him.

His partner, a twin brother possibly, just stood looking at him and the cabin.

What a moose! As we were getting off the roof, the second bull ran off into the willows making quite a racket as he headed north. We never saw that moose again.

Mae and I were breathless. I told her that this was likely the highest quality trophy animal either of us would ever take. We set about cutting it up, leaving the hide on the quarters as we removed each large piece to keep the meat clean.

When we had it field butchered, we enjoyed a hearty breakfast and then put a tape to the antlers. It measured sixty-five and one half inches in width, with twenty-two measurable points on each antler. It's palms were forty-nine inches in length and twenty-two inches wide. I had never seen another moose rack of such impressive dimensions. It was hard to take our eyes off of that trophy.

The next morning I removed the quarters from their hanging places and skinned them out before boning, then loading into the back of the cub. Next, I got the head, tied onto the right wing struts, and flew all of the meat but one back strap to Kotzebue and hung it in our meat cache. That was a real load for the cub, but it handled it well.

A mechanic friend of mine had an aluminum half barrel that he loaned me and I boiled the head with some difficulty, it being so huge. It took me

The best Moose (Alces alces gigas) that I've ever seen alive.

We dropped that huge bull right in our yard.

several days of intermittent boiling, then scraping, etc. Then I began to apply hydrogen peroxide to whiten the skull bones. The "European mount" turned out fine and I have that great rack in my living room still - nearly forty years later.

Two odd little cauliflower-like exostoses - exuberant bony growths - are in the middle of the skull, probably due to injuries sustained in rutting battles in a previous season.

A couple of years later an official Boone and Crockett Scorer was in Kotzebue and I had him score the head for us. At that time it placed about #16 in the book, but I noticed a significant error in his work, without which the score would have placed it in the top 5. Oh well.

Eight years later, an official Safari Club International measurer scored it, then had it verified by another and it was #5 in the SCI book. It is the most impressive trophy that I have ever participated in taking.

Over Turned Canoe and Booze

In September, 1977, heavy rain for several days had swollen the rivers, making gravel bar landings impossible. I had happened to fly over a huge bull moose, which was accompanied by several cows. Pre-rutting behavior was evident, so I felt certain that the band of moose would be nearby for some time. The moose were near the Kelly River, on the West side. The river would have to be crossed to get to them and to retrieve the meat. As we had not put our meat up for the winter, I planned to try to harvest that one, if and when conditions permitted.

My hunters at Trail Creek had been no more than inconvenienced by the high water as my air strip was a few feet above the local creeks and, more important, the lodge is so far up stream that in the more than forty years that I have been there, the strip has never been flooded. But thank Goodness for hip boots that allow us to access the surrounding country!

The rain stopped, the river level dropped and that made gravel bars once again usable. There was a five day gap between bookings and I knew a local fellow, Roger, who wanted to go hunting, so I invited him and he eagerly accepted. The deal was that whom ever got a crack at the big bull should shoot it and would keep the rack. The meat would be split evenly between us, as would the expenses and the work of packing out the meat.

After very little time, I located the big bull, which had gathered up a few more cows. I counted nine cows and three bulls in the group. Two smaller bulls had joined the crowd, hoping for an opportunity to jump a cow, if the big fellow was distracted.

We set up the tent, caught a fresh Arctic Char for supper and settled in for the night on a good gravel bar across the river from the moose.

In the morning, I inflated my rubber canoe and we paddled across the river without incident.

Heavy timber and fear of spooking the moose before we ever saw them kept our approach slow and cautious.

About a half mile from the river I saw the first cow and gave a short whistle to Roger. He glanced at me and I gave him the signal to proceed with ultimate caution. Roger nodded that he got the message.

The cow was browsing and soon we lost sight of her. I heard the sound of a stick cracking and thought it had been made by Roger, but instead, one of the smaller bulls came cruising by just forty yards in front of us. This was about a three year old bull and obviously had amorous designs on the cow. His upper lip was curled back in the flehming position, gathering the pheromones being emitted by the cow. Apparently this youngster decided that the cow was ready to accept his attentions and he made a short rush toward the area she had just walked through.

We heard the bull grunt followed by the sound of sticks and branches being crushed as the two moose ran further into the timber. She was not ready. Ah, the fickleness of females!

We heard more commotion ahead. Roger came to me and worried that the moose had smelled us or somehow sensed our presence. I told him that I doubted that, as there appeared to be no breeze and I expected that those two moose had startled others in the group. We remained where we stood for ten minutes.

After our pause, we again separated by about thirty yards and began to creep forward. The odor of moose hung in the still air.

Another twenty minutes of snail paced progress brought us to a small clearing. On the opposite edge were three cows and the big bull. He was standing partially concealed by branches and brush offering no clear shot.

A low whistle to Roger indicated he should stop. I was hoping that he would get an opportunity to dump the big bull, but later he told me that he never did see it.

One of the cows brought her head and ears up, reacting to my whistle. She looked around, then went back to nibbling on the browse.

A second cow turned our way and began approaching us from across the clearing. The bull racked his antlers through the branches, but did not follow the cow. I was dreading that the cow would come too close, sense

A "taker", but not the one I wanted.

us, and charge off, taking the big bull with her, but she turned and slowly ambled back toward the bull, to my great relief.

Time passed ever so slowly. The moose faded further back into the timber, so I whistled again, two short tweets, indicating that we should proceed.

As we neared the middle of the clearing I heard a bull grunt up ahead. Seconds later a cow came running from our left, up the middle of the open area, followed by one of the smaller bulls. I whistled one toot, indicating silence and not to shoot.

Suddenly to my left another big bull emerged from the vegetation. This was a certainly taker, but not the best I had seen that day. I gave a low whistle and waved my hand back and forth, indicating a negative to Roger.

Midway between Roger and I, the cow seemed to take alarm and turned to her left, entering the heavier timber with the young bull close behind her. The woods erupted with the sounds of brush breaking and hooves hitting the ground. Roger went forward into the trees. From the right side of the clearing, a large cow, followed by the big bull ran quartering toward me. I held for just behind the bull's jaw and squeezed. He dropped, as if pole axed, landing on his belly with all four legs underneath his body.

It was a spine shot.

I hollered " bull down", not wanting to have to deal with two moose that day. The work was about to begin.

If Roger had held his position he would have had a chance to shoot the bull, but I didn't mention that to him, as he said so himself.

We set to quartering the bull. I had my Hudson Bay ax tied to my pack board and after one side of legs were removed, I used the ax to chop free the ribs. The job is so much faster and easier to do with a good helper. The ax was used to remove the skull place and antlers as well. Normally I brought out the entire skull, then boiled it to make a European mount. This rack would go to Roger and he preferred to not have to do the boiling procedure. This decision of mine to chop the antlers free of the skull probably led to a mishap later that day.

The meat was tied on our pack boards, me with the two back straps, each eight feet long. Taken from behind the ears to the rump, they handle better and are easier to keep clean in just two large pieces. Roger brought out a haunch with bones removed and we headed for the canoe. The second trip had me taking the other hind while Roger took our a boned out front. The next haul was me with a front and Roger with the ribs. For the final trip, Roger packed out the antlers and I had the tenderloins, heart and liver -the lightest loads were saved for last.

With one hind and the smaller pieces in the canoe, I sent Roger across. One rope was in my hands for bringing the canoe back and a rope was to be kept on the other side for retrieval of the next load.

The next load was the other hind. These crossings were a bit tippy, with minimal freeboard, but the canoe was an inflatable, so Roger got his keister wet, however there seemed no danger of swamping the craft.

For the third trip I carefully placed the antlers and put in the two front quarters. As Roger pulled it across, the canoe dipped a little, allowing the lower shovels of the rack to catch in the current and the canoe flipped over. RATS! I saw the moose rack going down the river reminiscent of a paddle wheeler. The front quarters sank and disappeared. RATS!

Had I left the entire skull attached to the antlers, it likely would not have dipped and overturned the canoe. Oh well.

After getting the canoe back to me and the rest of the meat across the river, I got in the cub and flew to look for the two fronts and the rack.

The spine shot dropped the bull moose.

The Moose horns caught the current which rolled the canoe.

Good luck followed bad for us when I recognized two friends from Noatak in a skiff coming up the Kelly River. I landed nearby and learned that they had picked up the two front quarters and saw the rack hung in some sweepers a little way downstream. They figured there had been an accident and were coming up to help, dreading what they might find.

When they heard my story, they went back to get the antlers and brought them and the meat to us.

Well, our little mishap had a pleasant ending. My friends set up camp next to us, we had a great evening and I made two trips to Kotzebue with Roger and the moose the next day.

A week later, a local fellow, Errol, told me that after seeing my tire tracks, he had landed on the same gravel bar and shot one of the smaller bulls. However he had a Maule and could not tie the antlers on the wing struts to take to town. He asked me if I would get them for him. I agreed to do so, then he told me that he left his tent also, so, would I get that, too. I said that I would do it.

When I landed, my Noatak buddies were still hunting. In taking down the tent, I found a bottle of whiskey that was nearly half full. My friends came in from their hunt so I offered the bottle of whiskey to them. They gratefully accepted it.

Normally, if I had not needed to be flying, I would have had a snort off the bottle, too. But never before flying.

When I delivered the tent and moose rack to Errol, I mentioned that I had left the whiskey with the others.

Errol let out a moan. I wondered why he would be upset about that.

Errol told me that before departing, he and his buddy had peed into the whiskey bottle.

RATS!

When next I saw my friends from Noatak, I asked them how their trip had been. They said it was a great time and that they had run out of beer, so one evening, after the last beer was drained, they drank the whiskey that I had given them.

They must have been so high that they did not taste the "whiskey". And I never did tell them about it, either. Arggggh!

Howling up Wolves

Sometimes the most simple things can be so effective in hunting and fishing pursuits. Once on the way back home after a day of duck and pheasant hunting in Oregon I kept seeing Raccoons (Procyon lotor) crossing the rural road in front of me. I had eaten coon years before in Arizona and found it to be pretty palatable. I began wondering how one from this area might taste. Filbert orchards seemed to be attracting them, therefore the raccoons were no doubt feeding on the nuts. I distracted myself with wondering if the local coons might even have a nutty flavor.

Well, there was one obvious way to find out. I needed to harvest one and cook it up.

I pulled off the road near where a medium sized raccoon had just crossed. Seeing the animal humping along between the trees, he was already well out of range of my 12 gauge. Then he stopped and began to pick up nuts that had fallen. I eased over the barbed wire fence, scatter gun in hand. The coon saw me and began to run away. I barked like a dog, not expecting anything but an accelerated exit by the coon. But I was surprised to see it shinny right up the nearest tree. Astounded, I trotted to the tree and blew my supper off the branch.

Dumb coon, I figured.

Another mile further down the road, a similar scenario developed and I bagged another coon, using my dog barking technique. I had gained an invaluable piece of knowledge!

Those fourteen to sixteen pounders had dandy pelts, too!

I baked the first one up with some sliced onions, potatoes, carrots, beef broth and spices, and by golly, it was delicious. I had insured myself of now having a source of good eating protein treats any time of the year.

Normally I just carried a .22 pistol in the car and took advantage of this vulnerability of raccoons on numerous occasions over the next three years.

Discovering how easy it was to tree raccoons, I began fooling around with vocalizing while hunting other wild critters. Some of my efforts were met with success, some were not.

Hunting wolves in the springtime, a howl from me as we were skinning a shotgunned wolf, would often elicit a response from another wolf from the pack we had shot into, sometimes leading my partner and I to the addition of another pelt to the pile.

After the use of aircraft in hunting wolves was discontinued in Alaska, sightings of wolves became more frequent during summer and fall. It was not uncommon to hear them howl.

In 1996 I had taken three guest hunters from Florida, Tom, Rex and Henry, down creek to the South Overlook, searching for caribou and grizzly bears. The hunters each had a wolf tag, but we had not seen a lobo in more than a week of long days spent hunting the valley. As we were enjoying an afternoon break, I noticed a band of eight or ten Caribou coming rapidly up the creek on the opposite side of the valley. They were being pursued by two large gray wolves.

With nothing to loose, I let out a single long howl. The two wolves broke off their hot pursuit and made a ninety degree turn to the right toward us, stopping on a cut back at least a quarter of a mile away from where we sat. I let go with another long howl and the wolves came toward us on a run. The leader was bigger, which I assumed to be the male.

As the pair were coming through some pucker brush near Trail Creek, I told my guests to keep low and get set up, as I expected the wolves to come to the high bank below us, providing shooting at less than a hundred yards.

Henry was engaged in answering an urgent call of nature at that moment. Tom told him to hurry and get his pants pulled up and zipped, as the wolves were coming fast. It's funny how a sudden call to make haste will cause a man in such a situation to fumble, but you can count on it happening. Henry knocked his rifle off the rock it was leaning on and nearly fell down himself as he jittered with his zipper, finally abandoning his attempt to close his fly and joining us, barn door wide open, as we prepared for the appearance of the wolves.

"Put one up the spout and put your safety on," I whispered for all to hear

In what seemed like no time, the larger wolf popped up on the top of the bank, closely followed by the other.

Once again, they stopped and looked around. I did not call, as they were too close for that.

They put their noses close to the ground and began working their way up hill, toward us, stopping frequently to sniff the air and look around.

At about seventy yards I whispered, "Shoot, when ready."

Someone asked "Which one?"

"Rex, shoot the Left one, Tom the right, Henry your choice," I softly whispered.

Three shots rang out simultaneously, as if only one rifle had been fired.

Tom's wolf went down hard, the other turned and began leaping away, with all three men shooting at it. When it disappeared over the bank, I had not seen any sign of it having been hit.

In the meantime, Tom's wolf was up and running for the bank. The three shooters were all trying to stuff more rounds into their magazines, with fumbled shells falling to the tundra in the men's desperation.

I saw a large splotch of blood on the big wolf's mid section, but he was over the bank and out of sight in mere seconds.

We all four ran to the bank, scrutinizing the brush below. I saw blood on an open bit of sand and bailed off the ridge with the hunters. After several hundred yards of following the intermittent blood trail, Tom said he had to stop as he had something in his boot. It was a rifle shell that had been intended for his magazine.

We were able to trace that wounded wolf's escape for more than a mile. With so much blood, I expected to find it lying dead in its tracks, but instead, when its trail led to a cut bank of eight to ten feet in height, it continued straight on, up and over without sign of a pause. A badly wounded animal should not be able to do that. I figured that in spite of all the blood, the wound was not such a serious one.

After three hours we turned around and went back to the lodge without a wolf. We all felt really bad at loosing that critter. I lost a Grizzly bear in 1984 and now this wolf, the only animals I had been responsible for wounding and loosing to that date.

Three Shooters on 12 Wolves

Tom Minter, from the previous story and my good friend, joined us for hunts at Trail Creek several times, including 2001.

My sister, Pat and my commercial fishing partner, Tom Dooley were already in camp, as were Bob, the plumber (PlumbBob, I call him, of course).

My cousin Steve, had recently been honorably discharged from the Marines, after serving two hitches as a sniper. That kid could always shoot exceptionally well. I had to go to Kotzebue to pick up Steve. As I was returning to the lodge and beginning my descent to land I noticed several wolves lying in the pucker brush flat west of the South Overlook - about four miles down from the lodge. They showed no concern with the aircraft passing three hundred feet overhead. The way they were sprawled out, I suspected that they had just gorged themselves on some hapless prey animal. I counted twelve adult wolves.

Steve, having never seen a live wolf before was excited and gushed that we should go down there first thing tomorrow. I said that indeed, we would go to the overlook, but we should not expect to see any wolves, as they were apt to be miles away, in search of another ungulate with which to satisfy their voracious appetites, and stuff their bellies.

Next morning, Tom MInter, PlumbBob, Steve and I arrived at the South Overlook before lunch. Before finishing with our sandwiches, I spotted several wolves in the same section of dwarf birch they had been the evening before. We watched carefully with binoculars before determining that they were just loitering in the pucker brush about forty yards from the edge of the main channel of Trail Creek.

We discretely went back north to take advantage of better concealment terrane and the wind, which was gently drifting up creek, as we worked our way down to the creek. The day was warm for that latitude and we peeled down to T-shirts.

We verbally rehearsed the program. Everyone, except me, would put an extra round into the chamber as soon as we crossed the creek, to give each guest an extra shot, and put the rifle on safe. I would be crawling through the brush with PlumbBob and if the situation allowed, when I saw everyone in place, I would have Bob shoot whatever wolf was the furthest to the right and Steve was to shoot the furthest left. There were enough wolves, that Tom could take his pick of what was in between. Most important, I cautioned that all the wolves would react like a bombshell at the first shot, if not before, and each man should just shoot as many wolves as he could, without worrying about someone else shooting at the same critter. This action would very rapidly become a squeeze play, so lead in the air was the key to killing as many wolves as possible. Tom and Steve had tags and Bob, as an Alaskan resident could legally kill them all if the opportunity came his way, so we were covered.

The limit on wolves in that area is 20 per person per year. I would be very satisfied if each man got a single wolf, but here was a potential for multiples.

All had be totally quiet as we reached the edge of the brush. The men placed a round into the chamber, made the rifle safe and we began to slowly crawl through the dwarf birch brush. I was just a tad in front of Bob, often discretely peering up to try to see the wolves.

We located two gray wolves.

After about fifteen yards of slow progress I saw a gray female stand up and look around, obviously sensing something. We stopped crawling. I whispered to PlumbBob to get ready.

A second wolf, this one black, stood up to the left. It watched the gray which by then was showing some nervousness. When a third wolf rose I told PlumbBob to shoot the gray.

The gray wolf went down, as did the black one, the shots brought wolves jumping up out of the birches like popcorn from a skillet. The shooting was fast and mostly inaccurate, but I saw one more wolf react to a shot that found the target.

With so much action, I was trying to keep track of the wolves and missed a wonderful opportunity for some excellent video footage.

In a flash, the wolves were beyond reasonable shooting range and all were running hard, only occasionally showing the top of their backs as they sped away.

I told the shooters to all reload, but put nothing in the chamber until they had an opportunity for a shot. Then we got a collective inventory of who saw what. I saw the gray female and the first black wolf go down. I saw another gray shudder from taking a bullet. Two of the others said that a second large black had been dropped.

We spread out and began to search the waist high, dense brush from forty yards in front of us all the way across the pucker brush flat.

The four of us kicked the bushes for a full hour, finding only the large gray female and a smaller gray male. No dead black wolves were located. I am confident that our search was thorough as we did it in an organized fashion and I did find an Alaska Department of Fish and Game radio collar from a bear lying near a bush. No skin, bones or other sign of the bear was seen. I turned it in to the Alaska Department of Fish and Game and they confirmed that the bear was a male that I had assisted in catching, sampling and collaring on the North Slope in 1980 - twenty-one years and three months earlier.

It appeared that we had wounded and lost two black wolves. It's a rotten feeling that visits any ethical outdoors man when contemplating that he is responsible for wasting an animal's life, - worse yet that his prey has struggled off to suffer and possibly die a prolonged, miserable death.

We walked back to the lodge in a spiritual miasma of remorse. My life total was now four animals left in the field, three of which were wolves and all within a mile of each other, near the South Overlook on Trail Creek.

Two days later on a flight to town I saw a mob of wolves at Misheguk Creek, fourteen miles downstream from the lodge. I flew over them to make a count. There were eight. By the colors of the wolves, two blacks and six grays, I figured they were the same pack that had twelve members earlier that week when I had counted four blacks and eight greys. With the two grays we found and the two blacks that were seen absorbing a bullet, the tally was right. It is a real shame that we had been unable to locate the two blacks, but, like the big gray in 1996, they might have had the ability to go for miles before stopping.

Like all endeavors, hunting has some extremely disturbing realities - inevitabilities, if one is heavily involved for many years - even if pursued with the utmost legal and ethical standards. Loss of wounded game is the worst of all, in my view.

Kris' Wolves

In 2007, my grandson, Spencer and I hosted an interesting fellow. Kris was born in Tehran and he told me that he went back annually to visit relatives. He was a naturalized American citizen and a very pleasant man.

Kris was drawn for a Dall Ram permit on his first attempt and was ecstatic about coming for a sheep during the last ten days of August. As we were filling out the paperwork, I suggested that he purchase a wolf tag for thirty dollars, as Wolves are commonly seen and without a tag, he would have to use his $425 sheep tag on a wolf, but odds favored having the proper tag.

Kris told me that he wasn't much interested in a wolf, but he would buy a tag. The first wolf taken by our guest requires no trophy fee payment, so there is a huge incentive for all hunters to purchase the inexpensive tag.

The first day in camp, as we could not pursue any big game the same day airborne, we concentrated on fishing. Kris was adept with his fly rod, catching and releasing several Arctic Char and Grayling. He appreciated everything about the remote wilderness.

A positive attitude is always a cornerstone for a good time.

We were glassing sheep in all quadrants from the lodge windows. It appeared that selectivity would be wonderful. We decided to go north to check out Current Creek to evaluate rams in that drainage. A few Caribou were grazing here and there, but none were good trophy bulls.

That afternoon, after an enjoyable jaunt we three took our boots off and were enjoying a pleasant rest on a sunny hillside when Spencer said, "Grampa, there's a wolf!"

Sure enough, about a thousand yards up the creek a large gray wolf was engrossed with hunting lemmings on the same hillside we were on. The light breeze was drifting cross wind between us and the wolf.

We quickly booted up and using terrane to keep us invisible to the wolf, we closed the distance in a few minutes.

As we eased over the last contour, the wolf was still busy with rodents about 225 yards below us. The wind was gently coming from him to us. I told Kris that we dared not try to get closer, so he should take a rest and make the shot.

With plenty of time, I had my video camera rolling as he squeezed the trigger. It was a miss. The wolf immediately turned downhill and ran as hard as he could, broadside to us. Kris shot again and I was sure the wolf had been hit. It kept going and quickly disappeared into dense brush.

We went to the area and soon found the animal lying dead. The second shot had penetrated both lungs and severed the ascending aorta, but the Wolf had gone another fifty yards before collapsing. Wolves are tough.

It was a dandy big male. I estimated the age at five years or more - a full grown Arctic lobo that weighted approximately 120 pounds. Kris was happy that he had purchased a tag.

Upon returning to the lodge, I skinned the head and paws out of the hide, turned the ears, split the lips did a little fleshing before placing the skin in a tub of cool, lightly brined, creek water. August wolf skins are thinner than those taken later in the year and if salted too heavy, make tanning difficult. Over salted hides tend to tear, making the taxidermist's work that much more difficult.

There was no fresh meat for supper after this wonderful day, so I used ground venison for making spaghetti. I suggested that Kris buy another wolf tag, but he said he didn't think he could be so lucky that another opportunity would come his way, so he did not buy a second tag. I'm sure Murphy was listening.

Another beautiful day greeted us in the morning, so we hiked down Trail Creek toward Popple Creek.

Glassing from the lodge had revealed three rams on the southeast slopes, but as we traveled along the base of the incline, more sheep were sighted in several smaller canyons. At the head of the southernmost of the canyons were four rams, two of which appeared to be well over a curl.

Having most of the day remaining for the trip, and me with two artificial knees that had been surgically placed just five months before, we climbed at

Kris and his Wolf

a leisurely pace, enjoying the scenery and glassing the surrounding country as we went. Stopping to eat a sandwich at about 2500 feet above the valley floor, Spencer said "Grampa, I see another wolf."

A mature gray wolf was traveling north through the riparian area on our side of Trail Creek. Wolves two days in a row used to be a rarity, but with the currently high population, it has become something that we should be prepared to handle. Kris could not use his sheep tag and still hunt the rams we were after. Nevertheless, I gave a howl and the wolf abruptly stopped and looked our way. Another howl and it was trotting directly toward us. Kris was amazed at the wolf's reaction. We hunkered down and I got the video camera ready.

From our vantage point we could see the wolf from time to time as it made it's way up the slope. When it was out of sight below us, I howled a third time. Soon thereafter the wolf was standing broadside to us, downhill at about ninety yards. I filmed it as it stood looking around for more than a minute, before going back down to the valley floor. Once in the creek bottom it went directly to a fresh caribou kill in the dense brush that we had not noticed until the wolf began tearing at it. The predator worked at the carcass, feeding, for about twenty minutes, then, with a front quarter in it's mouth, it went back in the direction from which it had come. No doubt it had pups to feed.

A known wolf den is less than two miles from our position and has been in seasonal use for more than forty years.

We continued up the slope to investigate the four rams more closely. On viewing from the closer range, one of the group had a very good head, - much better than I had originally figured. After maneuvering into reasonable range - about 250 yards, Kris settled on the best ram and dropped it with his first shot.

My new knees were performing well, but the doctor had cautioned to take it easy on them and specifically to forego any sheep hunting this year. So, in partial deference to the sawbone's admonitions, I started back for the lodge as Spencer began caping and butchering the ram. This after all, was a training experience for Spencer during his assistance for me. We all gotta learn somehow, eh?

My trip back brought me within fifty yards of a Grizzly sow with two cubs, none of which was aware of my passing. A cow and calf caribou grazed on the runway and our resident weasel gave me a scolding, probably for coming back without meat as I opened the door of the lodge. Due to its behavior, I figured the weasel was probably a female.

I cooked up a stew and fed myself, then fell asleep in a chair in front of the main window. I woke up after dark to see Spencer and Kris' flashlights bobbing through the willows.

Inside, they told me that when darkness caught them, they decided to cache the trophy and meat, for retrieval the next day. Normally that is not a good idea, but different strokes, as they say.

We did recover the meat and head with cape the next day, but it took some searching. No bits of surveyor's tape had been used to direct them, or rather, us, back to their secreted cache. The wild country can be confusing to anyone, so I emphasized to them how important it is, if one must stash

Kris and his dandy Dall Ram.

08/27/2007

Kris and his Caribou, his third trophy of the trip.

something, to leave clear signs to help them locate it upon their return. This is even more important if someone else is to locate the spot. Small pieces of surveyor's tape tied to bushes are a great help in leading one to a cache, but of course the tape should be taken down once the object has been recovered.

We saw wolves several more times, but not again as close as the first two had been.

Kris decided to pursue a Caribou since he had several days left on his booking and good bulls had been coming down the valley daily.

Spencer had a softball tournament to participate in, so I took him to town and picked up Ron, my assistant guide from Colorado to finish out Kris' booking and stay through the September hunts.

We'd been looking over dozens of Caribou each day, but had not settled on a taker, until one evening just after supper. Three bulls were feeding across the valley and Kris liked the looks of one. I sent Ron with Kris, as I had some dishes and general clean up to do. I watched the men stalk and kill the animal from the kitchen window. As that was happening, a huge Grizzly was feeding on berries on the hillside just 200 yards from the opposite window. The big boar came into the yard, but ran away when I opened the window and hollered at him.

Frying bacon for breakfast the next morning I saw the same big bear I ran out of the yard the evening before. The bruin was feeding on berries as he ambled through the tussocks in front of the window. As I filmed the bear, I saw a large gray wolf watching the bear from a knoll. Soon the wolf was teasing the bear, which was becoming irritated. The wolf would run up close to the bear, then dodge away. This continued for about half an hour. I was able to film that and bits of the sequence are on my website. It was a wonderful conclusion to a most enjoyable ten days in the pristine Arctic wilderness, shared with great companions.

In December, 2008, Kris received impressive award plaques for his Wolf and Caribou, each of which placed number 2 in their categories. His sheep missed the top three, but, along with his memories, was his favorite trophy of all.

Polar Bear Hunting

Prior to coming to Alaska I had read lots of stories of hunting on the Last Frontier. Antlered game have always been my preference, but the ice bear was of special interest to me.

Reading that hunting Polar bears was the most expensive hunt in the world, (about $1,000 per bear hunt at that time) I expected that I would never engage in that, unless I could figure out a way to do it on my own. That would require that I take up residence in the far north and become a pilot. As airplanes cost several times what a decent boat would, I assured myself that a boat would be my means of transportation.

To my way of thinking, Polar bears were in the same category as the Bongo and Marco Polo sheep - way out of my potential range of possibilities.

In less than a year after arriving in Alaska I was co-owner of an airplane and had seen live Polar Bears. My dreams, hitherto always modest, had gone stratospheric!

Learning to fly under the tutelage of Babe Alsworth and his oldest son, Lonnie, I received my private license in 1969 and purchased a Cessna 180 in June of 1970. I struggled to keep my head…and my airplane out of the clouds.

Taking up residence in Kotzebue, then dubbed the "Polar Bear Hunting Capitol of the World," I resolved to collect one of the great bears, before the opportunities vanished. I suspected they soon would become more restricted or the already controversial hunt would be closed.

The speed of life was accelerating and I didn't want to be left entirely in the dust bowl of blown opportunities.

After owning the 180 for less than a year, in March, 1971, I was invited to "fly cover" for a couple of experienced Polar bear guides. The preferred air machine for flying the ice was a Piper Super Cub. A few guides got by with

Super Cruisers. But I heard of one guy using a Cessna 180. If I trimmed for slow flight in the Cessna, with two notches of flaps down, I could follow a cub adequately. It worked best if I stayed a bit higher and behind the smaller plane, keeping track of it and, with extra altitude, having less stress and strain. I soon learned that prolonged slow flight is very wearing on the pilot as the aircraft feels "mushy" and requires constant attention to avoid stalling. A full day of such flying is a really wearing experience. But I yearned for the experience and…for an ice bear. A nice bear, too.

The position of the active leads in the pack ice dictated where we went to look for the bears. Some days we flew down the coast of the Chukchi Sea toward Cape Prince of Wales, then west past the Diomede Islands and then headed north, following the open water. International law kept us three miles or further off the Siberian coast, lest we run into Soviet patrols.

Every day we would cross the International Date Line into tomorrow, then fly back across,…back into yesterday.

Bears were not usually hard to find. Their population was high. After a new snowfall, if the sunlight was good, fresh tracks stood out like lights. The older tracks did not appear nearly so brilliant and distinctive.

Sows and cubs were protected and hunters wanted big boars, anyway. Selectivity was maximized and few smaller bears or females were taken.

State regulations allowed one Polar bear per hunter, every three years, while for Brown and Grizzly bears the regulations allowed a bear every four years.

Though most of the Polar bear hunting took place in international waters, the hides and hunters had to return to Alaska where state regulations were in effect.

The man recognized as the best and safest bush pilot in NW Alaska, Warren Thompson, told me that he wanted to take a polar bear for himself or his son, Robert. If I was interested I could use my airplane to fly alongside him in his super cub and we would each try to collect a bear.

That was an offer I couldn't refuse.

Warren and I made a trip toward the Diomede Islands, then up the Siberian east coast and found only females with cubs, along with two freshly skinned carcasses. I was learning a lot about winter flying in the cold air over bright sunlit snow. Ice conditions and appearance require some getting used to and Warren was a great teacher. Good sunglasses were a must, along with appropriate clothing and plenty of extra fuel.

Two weeks passed before we could both fit in another personal trip. Warren suggested we go far to the Northwest, toward Wrangell Island.

Aviation fuel could be purchased in fifty-five gallon drums or five gallon sealed cans. For carrying along, the sealed cans were best. Fumes from leaky or refilled cans are horrible in the cockpit. I had twenty cans of avgas in the back of my Cessna and he had four cans in his cub. We each carried a passenger, a fuel funnel with a chamois, a catalytic heater, and engine cover, along with survival gear which included tents, heavy down sleeping bags and a snow knife for cutting hard packed snow to build a snow block (igloo) shelter if necessary. Of course we took plenty of food, enough to last for several days, - just in case.

On take-off we were loaded heavy.

We departed Kotzebue well before daylight, about 5:00 am and turned northwest, headed for Wrangel Island.

A thin overcast gave way to clear skies and unlimited visibility. The conditions were ideal for the task at hand.

We encountered a big lead not far offshore from Cape Krusenstearn. This open water stretch was at least five miles across so we both climbed our planes as we crossed. An engine failure over open Arctic water would be disastrous - almost certainly fatal. After crossing the big lead, we found mostly jumbled pack ice. Currents had shifted the ice and the smaller leads were blocked. We found old tracks, but had seen only three single bears, none of which would measure up to what we wanted.

Shortly after noon, within sight of Wrangel Island, we landed to stretch, pour fuel in the tanks, and have another cup of coffee. It seemed the best idea to turn back and hunt our way toward home. We would fly a route more to the East to avoid retracing our outbound path in hopes of finding some active leads and some good bears.

Another two hours of finding no open leads was discouraging. As we were going along with me behind at about 1500 feet and Warren close to 600 feet above the ice, I saw some darker color ahead and then there was movement! Several bears, with their white coats stained a yellowish brown color were coming out of a hole in the ice. I radioed to Warren describing what I saw. He replied "that is no hole, that's a wishing well".

Ten Polar bears came out onto the ice from the dark hole. The afternoon sun was getting low on the horizon and shadows were lengthening, so we had to act fast, if we were to do anything.

The nearby ice pans were not ideal, actually they were pretty rough. There was one narrow strip of snow covered ice that looked doable, so Warren dropped his flaps and went in. I noticed his cub took a serious pounding before he got it stopped.

Warren landed first and I flew lazy circles in the area away from where we wanted the bears to go.

Several bears came running at high speed from the darkened area, climbing over a pressure ridge of broken ice, to the pan were Warren and his son, Robert, were waiting. I saw one big bear go down.

I studied the landing spot. It did not look inviting, but with the narrowing window of opportunity for taking a Polar bear, I decided to give it a try. I picked a place a bit closer to the bear hole. One landing area had a dog leg in it, but was a good 300 feet longer and didn't look any rougher than other nearby options, so that's where I touched down. The airplane made snapping and popping noises as it hit the ice ridges, but it slowed down rapidly after I dumped the flaps. Normally I would not have put down in such a gnarly place. I was glad I had replaced the factory landing gear with the heavier Cessna 185 gear.

I taxied close to Warren's cub and asked him to get airborne and bring a bear back to me.

He got in the cub and began to fly low and slow near the dark area. After ten minutes, three Polar bears were coming my way. I was disappointed to see that one had fresh blood on it's front shoulder. It was not the largest of the three, but was obviously wounded, so I shot it.

Well, I had my Polar bear.

Time was short, but we had to see what was in the hole that had given birth to ten Polar bears. We walked up and clearly saw that it was a whale, probably a bowhead, frozen into the ice. The bears had been eating it out, working like coal miners. It smelled like whale and not rotten at all. The bears had been rubbing up against the blubber, which gave them a more yellowish color than normal.

No one had a good quality single lens reflex camera along, but we made some hasty pictures with what we had and got at skinning the two bears.

We'd burned a lot of fuel, making both planes much lighter than they'd been when we left town which was a good thing considering the short, rough area available for take-off.

I put both hind quarters of my bear in the back for eating and sharing with neighbors. Few Polar bear hunters brought any meat at all back to town which seemed unconscionable to me. Local Eskimos loved polar bear meat.

We were ready to depart that ice pan just at sundown. We were so far away that my ADF could not pick up the Kotzebue beacon on its 356 frequency. Remembering that wide lead, we headed for where we believed we would find Point Hope or Cape Thompson, neither of which had radio navigation aids.

Lights from Point Hope village were a welcome sight. We steered a bit to the right and followed the coast, cutting directly over the lower lend of the Noatak River once the ADF was locked on to the Kotzebue non-directional beacon. We landed after midnight. It had been a long day.

The next weekend was blustery and overcast, not good weather for anyone to be on the ice. A guide friend asked me to meet him at the local speakeasy called Stubby's coffee house. Kotzebue was officially a "dry" town, but for an extra dollar, Stubby would lace your mug with a shot of rot gut whiskey.

That little dive was packed with polar bear guides, hunters and taxidermists, and as usual, things were pretty loud and boisterous.

Someone mentioned that I had brought some bear meat to town and another guide said that eating polar bear liver would kill you. Truth is, polar bear liver is so highly concentrated with Vitamin A, that you could die of hypervitaminosis if you ate a lot of it, over a prolonged period of time.

A taxidermist from Spokane suggested that I might enjoy eating some nice Polar bear liver. He'd been sipping Stubby's rot gut for too long, or so it appeared to me from his slurred talk. I suggested that, indeed, I might enjoy that sort of meal.

He offered to bet me $500 that I would not eat Polar bear liver. I suggested that he then bring me one and shook his hand in front of the crowd. As we shook hands, I emphasized for all to hear that I would eat Polar bear liver, not "a" Polar bear liver.

The next week the guy called me and said he had the liver, asking if I had the $500 in cash, as he expected me to croak before he could cash a check. I agreed to meet him at Stubbys at 7:00 pm with cash in hand.

It was standing room only if one kept his arms tight to his body when I arrived. I showed my $500 in cash, and so did the taxidermist.

There on the bar counter lay a huge lobe of Polar bear liver. I asked if he was sure of what it was. He said he cut it out himself. It was unmistakably a piece of liver. I cut off a large chunk and cooked strips of it on Stubby's hot plate. Then I chewed and swallowed a piece about the size of a walnut - just enough to satisfy everybody and offered them a chance to taste some. Not one of them would eat any - not even a little nibble.

After a few more rounds of rot gut, with me still on my feet and showing no signs of discomfort, the taxidermist paid me and I went home, still upright and $500 richer.

That was a case of somebody hearing something, not checking it out and getting them self in trouble.

Later that same spring I went down to Stubby's with another guide buddy and as we sat at the counter telling jokes, that same taxidermist mentioned in his slurred speech that Stubby's cat seemed to be sick. The big yellow, long haired Tomcat was lying on top of the juke box that was throbbing out loud music.

The animal stuffer guy said that he suspected the cat was constipated.

One of the visiting hunters said that he was a veterinarian and had a cure for the cat He picked the cat up and headed across the street to the garage used by the taxicab.

The crowd followed.

The wind was blowing making the chill factor somewhere around - 70 degrees below zero. It was bloody cold.

Inside the garage was a hygrometer used for checking antifreeze level. It's bulbous squeeze end was protruding from a coffee can which contained some liquid.

The poor old cat began to struggle to escape, but the Vet, with the feline under his arm, tightened his grip. With the cat under one arm, freeing his other hand to do whatever he had planned. He had good control of the animal.

The Vet sucked up the liquid in the bottom of the coffee can, inserted the hygrometer tube into the cat's behind and gave the bulb a squeeze.

That yellow cat let out a horrendous screech, leapt free and zipped around the interior of the garage two times before making another hideous sound and flopped over on it's back with all four legs stuck straight up in the air. Every hair on that cat was as stiff and outstanding as it's legs. It looked like an expired porcupine.

After a period of violent shuddering, the cat was still.

I looked in the coffee can and smelled the contents. It was gasoline!

So now, reader, are you wondering if the cat was dead?

When people hear this story told orally, the usual, disgusted response is "So, did the cat die?"

The answer is, "No, he just ran out of gas."

That's the sort of story that may be developed when a bunch of guys are sitting around waiting for weather to improve and have too much time on their hands.

⚜

After passage of the Marine Mammal Act, I made a couple more trips to observe and photograph the ice bears. We flew a few miles west of Cape Krusenstern and found plenty of active leads. One one occasion in late March we saw a large boar following a smaller female. It seemed the male was looking for love. Polar bears usually travel in a straight line, so we landed the two planes about a mile ahead of the bears and concealed ourselves in a broken pressure ridge bordering a large flat ice pan and waited.

The bears appeared at the far end of the pan and continued in our direction, walking right up the middle of the flat ice. About 100 yards from us, the big boar looked directly at us, then abruptly turned it's head back toward the sow's tail. The boar began sidestepping, edging closer to us. He did not look directly at us again, but seemed to be keeping track of us and was definitely coming closer with every step.

It gave me an eerie feeling.

My partner stood up and waved his mitten, I pushed a round into the chamber of my ever present rifle. The boar kept coming. I stood up and yelled as did each of our passengers. Seeing four jumping, noisy people, the big bear hesitated. The sow wheeled to her left and took off at a gallop, which was too much for the boar. He followed her, casting glances back at

Polar Bears hunt the open leads for seals.

My bear had been wounded.

Warren, Robert, Ray and the first
bear of the day.

Jim Cann and guests with
a really big Polar Bear.

us as he ran. His actions seemed to indicate that love trumps war, in *Ursus maritimus*, at least.

Thinking about this and other incidents, I believe the Polar bears are the most intelligent of bruins - and the most dangerous.

Anyway, I've run out of gas telling cat and Polar Bear hunting stories, so that's it - for now.

WALRUS...or Waterus?

Sometimes I wonder how the devil an animal got dubbed with the name it carries. Anyone can see how appropriately a Warthog is named. Same for a Cloudy Leopard. Rattle snake, that's obvious. Sperm whale...well.... But Walrus...it seems that should be applicable only to members of the species that have been placed on a plaque, then hung on a wall in someone's trophy room. When those great beasts are in the ocean, I always thought they ought to be called Waterus.

While in Anchorage in February, 1968, the Alaska Dental Director of the Indian Health Service told me that the Nome dentist did not want to make the field trip to St. Lawrence Island and since my rural village work was already done, he wondered if I would volunteer to make the visits to Gamble and Savoonga.

I said that I would certainly be willing to make that trip which was scheduled for March.

Geography was always interesting to me and that of Alaska was especially so. I had a mental picture of where it was that I had volunteered to go, but wanted more detailed information.

That night I went to the library and read all I could find about St. Lawrence Island. I learned that it was populated by Siberian Yupik Eskimos who speak a language different than that of the Inuit or Yupik peoples of mainland Alaska.

The island is only 58 miles from the Chuckchi Peninsula of Siberia and about three times that far from Nome, Alaska.

It is the sixth largest island in the United States and the 113th largest in the world at 90 miles long and 8 to 22 miles wide. Currently with only two villages, Gamble and Savoonga, and a Distant Early Warning site operated by the U.S. Air Force at Northeast Cape, it was sparsely populated.

Vitus Bering visited the island in August, 1728. This was the first place in Alaska known to have been visited by Europeans.

Large sea mammals such as Whales, Walrus, Seals and Polar Bears provided most of the food for the villagers, supplemented with Reindeer meat after their introduction to rural Alaska in the 1800s.

This island intrigued me and I felt fortunate at being offered the opportunity to go there to provide dental care to the local people.

My dental field routine was to begin with school kids as soon as classes started in the morning, take a half hour to choke down whatever was on the school lunch menu for the day, then resume working at the dental chair until 5:00 pm or later. After an hour break for supper, which sometimes included a short nap, I was back at my dental stool until everyone who showed up had been seen, which usually took until ten in the evening or later. If the dental needs were being met, I sometimes took off Sunday morning and evening but often worked those periods as well.

I put out my best effort every day, including weekends, and the people appreciated it, often suggesting that I should not work so long and hard. Many times I was invited to join the villagers in their activities which ranged from enjoying a natural hot spring soak to going hunting or fishing with them. I had to defer most invitations, but was able to make time for some of those new and interesting activities.

After a week at Savoonga, I had caught up the entire school population's dental needs and even run out of adult requests for care. We were due to be flown to Gambel, but the weather was too sour for the aircraft to get in from Nome, so I polished up my pinocle game, played some pool and read, remaining packed and ready. After several frustrating days of waiting, I arranged with some of the locals to take us by skin boat to Gambel. The assistant traveling with me at the time was not keen on my idea. She'd grown up in King Cove, a coastal village on the Alaska Peninsula, and knew a lot more about Alaskan maritime conditions and the potential for weather deterioration, than I did, but the decision was mine to make and she reluctantly helped load her bag, along with the crates of government field dental gear into the 24 foot boat.

This boat was of unique construction. Split walrus skins were sown together and laced over the driftwod frame. Local sewers made water tight stitches where the skins needed to be larger. Those skins were naturally water proof and had a soft texture when wet, - almost like gum rubber. Young ice can cut through wood, fiberglass or aluminum, but the soft skin is impervious to being cut by ice. It's the only way to float around Arctic sea ice.

We encountered many "Waterus" enroute to Gamble.

The boat was powered by a 35 hp Evinrude and paddles were stowed onboard.

We set off for Gambel, seeing many pods of walrus along the way. Then, several hours into the journey, a dark storm front suddenly appeared, rapidly baring down on us. Waves began to build, causing the ice pans to jam and bob around. We were forced to turn back for Savoonga. Before regaining solid, shore fast ice the head man decided it best to haul the boat up onto a huge pan of thick floating ice to wait for calmer conditions.

My assistant was not happy. She had that "I told you so" look on her face.

Our situation seemed dire as we watched the ice pans, driven by wind and currents, close off the open tracts of water which are called "leads."

After more than three hours of waiting on the large ice pan, stomping our feet to keep our toes tolerably warm, watching the chunks of ice cut and grind against each other, sometimes piling high into the air, sometimes noisily collapsing, a narrow channel developed, allowing us to launch and slowly make our way toward land. Visibility was less than a mile in blowing snow, but the captain had a hand held compass, by which he directed our travel. At times we moved only a few yards before the two men at the bow were forced to use their long poles to push aside great pieces of floating ice to allow us to proceed. Often they would jump over the gunnel and manipulate the boat while standing on floating ice. The outboard motor was useless in such conditions, but the paddles sufficed.

The sun disappeared and with the heavy overcast, we were left in deep darkness. And it was cold.

Thank God for the compass! At my first opportunity, I would add a reliable one to my kit and forever keep it handy on all my travels.

We made it to fast (frozen to the shore) ice near the village, at midnight. Everyone was soaked, chilled and grateful for this deliverance.

Our gear was unloaded, transported back to Savoonga and stacked back in the warm clinic.

My assistant was silent, avoiding eye contact with me. She was boiling with anger, and she had been thoroughly frightened.

The morning brought sunlight through the now broken cloud layer and I was ready to make another attempt to reach Gambel. However, my assistant threatened mutiny if I forced the issue of a second attempt by boat, so we waited for the plane. Federal civil servants can be difficult at times.

One morning three men from the village came by and asked if I would like to join them on a walrus hunt. They said that if I could hit a walrus in the head, I could have the tusks and nose bone. What an offer! I nearly choked with joy as I accepted it, asking what I could bring.

"Bring your rifle", they said.

In those days, I always carried my Husqvarna 30:06 and a twelve gauge shotgun in my home made plywood case. I had packed some military solid nosed bullets, which would be perfect for walrus head shots.

Waving to my assistant, as she looked on with apprehension and disgust, we set off in the same skin boat that had borne us so admirably on our attempt to reach Gambel.

This trip was not to be such a long one. We encountered several groups of walrus within sight of the village. The tiller man turned off the kicker and four men silently paddled to within fifty yards of the pod of walrus.

The rifle's barreled action had cost me sixty dollars while I was still in dental school and the walnut stock blank, another five bucks. After more than forty hours of cutting, trimming gouging, fitting, sanding and rubbing, I had a beautiful rifle, - the first really good rifle I had ever owned.

Nathaniel, the head man, asked me if I thought I could hit a big bull in the head. I told him that I believed I could do so.

When the bull I wanted turned his head sideways to me, I aimed just behind the eye, and squeezed. The head dropped to the ice. It was a brain shot!

This one nearly slipped away.

Nathaniel hollered, "shoot some more, Doctor!" So I brained another bull before it could get off the pan of ice and everyone whooped for joy. I hollered, too.

The bull walrus would have weighed in at over a ton each, and this activity was a ton of fun for me, too.

The eskimos cut those two big bulls up and loaded them into the boat. Large sections of skin were removed and taken for sale. They would eventually be prepared for use in polishing jewelry.

When the belly was opened, steam formed above the warm insides and I watched as the men sorted through the innards of the animal. Soon they had their hands full of fresh calms retrieved from the stomach.

I enjoyed a mouthful of fresh clams, right out of a walrus stomach! That's the primary method of getting clams in this Arctic area. A little lemon and seasoning would have improved the taste, but it was good… and warm, as served.

But the limit, then under State control, was four walrus per boat per day, The skin boats could carry the load and the game was close at hand, so we took two more bulls. Those were shot by others in our party.

Butchering Walrus to load into skin boat.

What a day it had been! I had not remembered to bring any lunch, but Nathaniel offered me some of the food that he and the crew were eating which included boiled walrus meat with fat and skin attached - a hairy entree pronounced "Coke". I ate it gladly, along with some Agutuk, or eskimo ice cream made by mixing caribou or reindeer fat with small bits of cooked meat or berries. It's very calorific and a perfect meal for a cold day full of physical exertion and emotional elation.

"I feel like I'm in Hog Heaven" I said, but my comment drew quizzical stares from the eskimos. I explained the hog heaven bit, but it was lost in the cultural chasm. Oh well. No offense intended and none was taken.

Man, did I enjoy that day in 1968! I was 25 years old and Alaska was proving to be far better than my wildest dreams had forecast.

After 3 more days of waiting, the plane from Nome arrived. Indian Health Service headquarters radioed to the school that due to the long delay, we should cancel the trip to Gamble and return to Nome. After one night in the old gold rush town which included a hamburger for a whopping five dollars, we boarded a mail plane for Shaktoolik in Norton Bay.

In 1972, the Marine Mammal Act made it illegal for anyone but coastal dwelling Alaskan Natives to take any sea mammals, including Polar Bear, Walrus, the various species of Seals and Whales.

My adventure was closed to others with passage of the law.

Getting Right with the Lord

I've always been proud to be a Christian, though imperfect, and an unabashed, flag waving, patriotic American, but disparaging or cynical comments for either of those characteristics, coming from others, have perplexed and confused me since I was first confronted with them decades ago. Sometimes I even get a bit angry at such words, and given the opportunity, I am always ready to present the other side of the story.

Religion wise, I have no problem with those who follow different doctrines. I've been blessed with many good friends from different faiths from Jews to Mormons and most everything in between.

However, I've always been prone to soap boxing about American exceptionalism and am not at all tolerant of the "blame America first" crowd. I have always felt so lucky to be born an American and I make no bones about it.

And I thank God for it.

As far as I'm concerned, if a person is true to their faith and not too flagrant a hypocrite, that's fine with me. As I see it, we're all hypocrites to some degree, so some self examination now and then is a good idea. One shouldn't let his or her own hypocrisy go completely unchecked.

Similarly, a person can be a teetotaler or an imbiber of alcoholic beverages, so long as the drinker handles it appropriately - meaning they don't get in the face of those in their company or put anyone, including themselves, at risk.

I figure we all are at least ten percent crazy and should feel greatly blessed if our ten percent isn't smeared all over the surface, like a veneer, for everyone to see right away.

As a matter of fact, regarding alcohol, I often enjoy a glass of wine with dinner and/or a shot of whiskey sitting around after the dishes are done. A little alcoholic alchemy can lubricate the lips, often liberating some entertaining tales with which to pass the ever lengthening autumn evenings in hunting camps.

In Arctic Alaska we loose about eight minutes each day in September - that makes for about an hour more of darkness with each passing week, so some friendly, funny palaver is always welcome. John Barleycorn and his kin have loosened tongues and firmed friendships since man first discovered fermentation. Amen.

In my contracts and written instructions I remind guests to bring their own choice of booze, - and in sufficient quantity to carry them through their time away from liquor vendors, if they are so inclined. The lodge is a long way from the nearest liquor store, for sure. But few bring enough.

Nope, most commonly, guest hunters don't bring enough libation makins to wet their whistle with even a little touch each day, but many sure feel the need of it, once they're in camp. Even fewer of my guest hunters have ever brought enough booze to leave a little behind when they departed - and one fellow had to make a satellite phone order, ship extra elixir up via Alaska Airlines Gold Streak, then charter a plane to the lodge, so he would have enough of his preferred fire water. Now, THAT was expensive whiskey! At least he anticipated his soon-to-be shortage before things became critical for him.

Maybe folks figure they will go on a self disciplined period of abstinence while in hunting camp, but the fresh air, interesting and sometimes exciting experiences, new sights, tastes and company all lead to packing away a lot of lunch, and usually some extra grog. We've never run clear out of edibles yet, though.

When the day is at its closing, for most guest hunters, those wonderful, wild, natural stimuli call for quenching with some liquid spiritual refreshment. There's no sense in coming unprepared for whatever eventuality may arise. Snake bite medicine should be carried in sufficient supply on every trip, by those who indulge in this age old communal ritual. It's a glum camp that runs out of mosquito repellent, toiler paper, food or drink.

To be prepared for a paucity of hootch, should it develop, as it most commonly does, I stock a few extra bottles under my bunk, and out of sight, until absolutely needed.

Having a personal preference for whiskey or bourbon, while making my way North, I stop by the discount houses in Anchorage or Fairbanks and purchase some 1.75ml bottles of whatever decent squeezin's I can find. Often Lord Calvert is available at a reasonable price, so I grab a jug or two of that. I keep a bottle of it around just for fun, too.

When the guest's bottles have gone dry, I like to humbly suggest that after a wonderful day in such an outstanding example of God's unsurpassed creativeness, that maybe it's time we all "get right with the Lord". That comment often elicits an emotional withdrawal, or even a physical recoil, by some parties.

Some seem to suddenly have no neck.

Their relief when I produce the Lord Calvert container is amusing. It's worth a little extra in purchase price.

Getting right with the Lord.